I have always longed to be a part of the outward life, to be out there at the edge of things, to let the human taint wash away in emptiness and silence as the fox sloughs his smell into the cold unworldliness of water; to return to the town as a stranger. Wandering flushes a glory that fades with arrival.

- J.A. Baker, from *The Peregrine*

HERON DANCE

(802) 388-4875 Toll free (888) 304-3766

•

E-mail: heron@herondance.org
Website: www.herondance.org

•

•

ISSN 1532-9542

•

Periodicals postage paid at Middlebury, VT and additional mailing offices.
HERON DANCE (USPS 19-331) is published quarterly by Heron Dance Limited
52 Seymour St.
Middlebury, VT 05753-1115
Annual Subscription $25

•

POSTMASTER:
Send address changes to
HERON DANCE, 52 Seymour Street,

Contents:

Watercolors and photographs by Rod MacIver except the work on pages 17, 18, 19 and 54 by Ladislav Hanka and pages 58 and 61 by Ann O'Shaughnessy.

I like to walk about amidst the beautiful things that adorn the world.

- George Santayana

Auntie made me believe we live in a discoverable world, but that most of what we discover is an unfathomable mystery that we can name – even defend against – but never understand.

- Harry Crews, from *Getting Naked with Harry Crews*

Subscriber Letters

A year ago I received a Heron Dance flyer. I recall with some clarity following up with a phone call late at night. To my surprise the phone was answered by Rod MacIver, editor. We talked about canoe country with a mutual affection and reverence. Shortly afterwards, Heron Dance started coming to our home.

The latest and late edition just arrived. The delay was no special hardship and I found joy again in the strange and marvelous mix of material in this edition. In the time I have been a faithful reader, the issues have gotten better and better. And this latest version is the best!

Everyone should purchase a publication which has no advertising just for the sake of perpetuating such a marvel. But Heron Dance goes farther. It feeds those of us who have a contemplative streak, who find a measure of meaning and value in thinking, reflecting and meditating. But I might be biased from thousands of miles paddled!

Keep up the good work.

Love and peace, Jerry Ebbinga

Heron Dance continues to reawaken childlike wonder in me, nourish my soul, and send me out to SEE in ever deepening ways. Both "heron", and "dance" are soul symbols I resonate with and aspire to live. Heron is important to me for her innate wisdom and self reliance. And I have always loved to dance and have come to recognize and participate more consciously in the Great Dance we are all invited to join.

Heartfelt thanks to you, my friend, and to others like Frederick Franck, whom you have introduced to your readers, for your and their commitment to artistry, beauty, and the wonder of the natural world. Your labors of love radiate out as healing energies to our wounded and sacred – yet scarred planet – the living body of our HOME here on earth.

With gratitude and blessing, Fran

I received my first issue of your publication today (issue 29). The watercolors are wonderful but it only took me a minute or two to realize that your work was not for me.

I am, therefore, asking that you cancel my subscription.

May your path be smooth and may those who find your work interesting multiply tenfold.

- Georgiann Carlson

I have been enriched and encouraged by all the folks, thoughts and viewpoints expressed in Heron Dance. People on the front lines, engaged love in action.

But I have to say I was very disturbed by the suicide of, I believe, Virginia Hine in issue 29. It seems to me like a waste and supreme folly to off yourself to see what's on the other side. Death comes soon enough. It seems particularly strange that other people thought it was a good idea! How conscious can you be if you go out on drugs and alcohol?

Smacks of "Heavens Gate". Do you think she boarded the spaceship?

Aghast and horrified, Theresa Almario

Hi! I am renewing for another year – but so far don't really understand the purpose or mission of your magazine – nor does my friend who has also recently subscribed. I had thought your magazine and the writing would inspire me spiritually, but the first issue confused me. It appeared the writer is only satisfying his own needs.

- Name withheld

Heron Dance *started out as work for change. I tried to espouse a spirituality, but the words came slowly and were often contradictory. Over time, our goals have become simpler. We want to create a watercolor journal inspired by a love of wild nature, and do that as beautifully as we can.*

- Editor

I just received my first issue (#29) of Heron Dance. It was kind of strange at first. I didn't know what to expect. I read the subscriber letters and wondered what I was getting myself into. Some comments sounded mean and others sounded amazingly wonderful and from the heart. I have my own personal causes and I'm a positive person and so I read on. Well... I'm not sure how to express what I have read. I LOVED IT! I liked some things more than others, but truly loved it all. How very neat! What a joy to know that people think of nature and of life and have aspirations, do soul searching and have wonderful meaningful thoughts, oh, and can share them. How very awesome!! I can't wait for the next issue. I feel so very lucky to have found you. Thank you!

Sincerely, Wendy Salick

I have so appreciated the subscription to Heron Dance – it is a beautiful reminder to slow down and to go within.

I live in NYC where the lifestyle and tempo are astonishing. Everything moves at light speed. The mindfulness it requires to live in harmony while moving forward amongst the chaos is very different from the solitude a mass of trees offer. Here the large buildings and cement beneath my feet bring a staccato rush of exhilaration. Sometimes it is wonderful and sometimes it leads to a false sense of importance. People get wound into the money and the doing. Being is knowing who you are – who you are is your heart and the way you love with it, not what you do. I thank you for reminding me of this, of the importance of a simple walk in Central Park or of leaving the city for a ride in my dad's boat, where we watch fish flip and forget about the skyscrapers for a while.

Thank you, Julia Klein

I have always danced through life – all 72 years of it – and now that your publication has joined me, my dance is more joyful and I find myself, like Ginger Rogers, dancing backwards and in high heels.

God bless the two of you, and your crew, and stay well.

Edie Wolfe-Brown

I applaud your courage to focus Heron Dance on wild nature, the joy and passion of your life. This in itself is a recipe for personal success, regardless of material measures such as subscription renewals.

Inspiring people to embrace our common realization of the beauty of wild nature is a softer approach, but one with great potential impact. It is different than trying to change the world through overt efforts. There's nothing wrong with admitting that you hope to have a favorable impact on humanity, even if it's ancillary to your primary passion of just sharing the beauty you feel.

Your quotes of Robert Hénri and Vincent Van Gogh in issue 30 seem to get at the heart of the issue, and they reflect introspective courage.

How nice to see the wonderful, simple, peaceful, passionate focus coming to your life. Kudos to you.

Your friend, Hal Eastman

I am cutting out my subscriptions to many magazine this year, but not Heron Dance. It touches a deep, quiet place within that always needs nourishing! Please continue – the world sorely needs this message!

Blessings, Carol C. Daugherty

Please renew my subscription to Heron Dance. I really enjoy the magazine. It is always uplifting and spiritually reviving. OK, so a little schmaltz never hurt anyone. Some people don't put syrup on their pancakes either.

The watercolor paintings are beautiful and exquisitely rendered.

Best regards, Carol Page

Letters: We welcome reader feedback. If you would rather we did not print your letter or e-mail, please indicate. Space limitations require the editing of some letters.
Submissions: We have no submission guidelines and rarely publish unsolicited submissions. If you have read two issues of Heron Dance and have work you would like to recommend or share please send via postal service rather than e-mail.

What we may miss in human interaction here we make up for by rubbing elbows with wild animals. Their florid, temperamental lives parallel ours, as do their imperfect societies. They fight and bicker, show off, and make love. I watched a bighorn ram in rut chase a ewe around a tree for an hour. When he caught and mounted her, his horns hit a low branch and he fell off. She ran away with a younger ram in pursuit. The last I saw of them, she was headed for a dense thicket of willows and the old ram was peering through the maze looking for her.

When winter comes there is a sudden population drop. Frogs, prairie dogs, rattlesnakes, and rabbits go underground, while the mallards and cinnamon teal, as well as scores of songbirds, fly south because they are smarter than we are. One winter day I saw a coyote take a fawn down on our frozen lake where in summer I row through fragrant flowers. He jumped her, grabbed her hind leg, and hung on as she ran. Halfway around the lake the fawn fell and the coyote went for her jugular. In a minute she was dead. Delighted with his catch he dragged her here and there on the ice, then he lay down next to her in a loving way and rubbed his silvery ruff in her hair before he ate her.

- Gretel Ehrlich, from *The Solace of Open Spaces*

It is interesting, the debris in the air. A surprising portion of it is spider legs, and bits thereof. Spider legs are flimsy, Oxford writer David Bodanis says, because they are hollow. They lack muscles; compressed air moves them. Consequently, they snap off easily and go blowing about. Another unexpected source of aerial detritus is tires. Eroding tires shed latex shreds at a brisk clip, say the folks who train their microscopes on air. Farm dust joins sulfuric acid droplets (from burned fossil fuels) and sand from the Sahara Desert to produce the summer haze that blurs and dims valleys and coasts.

We inhale "many hundreds of particles in each breath we take," says Bodanis. Air routinely carries intimate fragments of rug, dung, carcasses, leaves and leaf hairs, coral, coal, skin, sweat, soap, silt, pollen, algae, bacteria, spores, soot, ammonia, and spit as well as "salt crystals from ocean whitecaps, dust scraped off distant mountains, micro bits of cooled magma blown from volcanoes and charred microfragments from tropical forest fires." These sorts of things can add up.

At dusk the particles meet rising water vapor, stick together and fall; that is when they will bury you. Soil bacteria eat what they can and the rest of it stays put if there's no wind. After thirty years, there is a new inch of topsoil. (Many inches of new top soil, however, have washed into the ocean.)

- Annie Dillard, from *For the Time Being*

And there is a Catskill eagle in some souls that can alike dive down into the blackest gorges, and soar out of them again and become invisible in the sunny places.
- Herman Melville

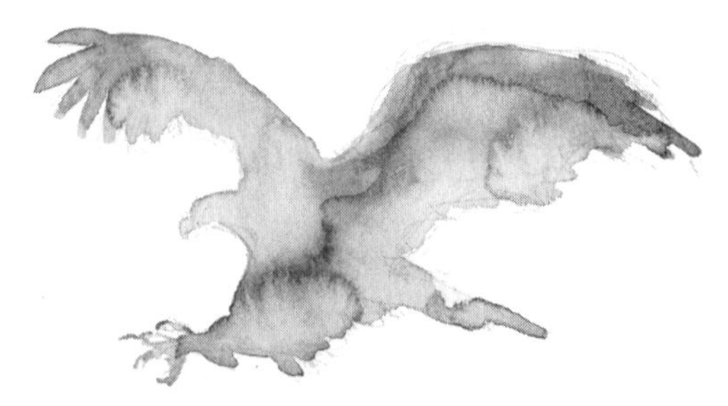

eagles in the rain

young eagles circling over the river
winding round the pines
in the rain   I did not think
they would come out into it
but they have   and now they dive
down   shooting through the ravines
- Robert Schuler

I came late to the love of birds. For years I saw them only as a tremor at the edge of vision. They know suffering and joy in simple states not possible for us. Their lives quicken and warm to a pulse our hearts can never reach. They race to oblivion. They are old before we have finished growing. . . .

For ten years I spent all my winters searching for that restless brilliance, for the sudden passion and violence that peregrines flush from the sky. For ten years I have been looking upward for that cloud-biting anchor shape, that crossbow flinging through the air. The eye becomes insatiable for hawks. It clicks towards them with ecstatic fury, just as the hawk's eye swings and dilates to the luring food-shapes of gulls and pigeons.

- J.A. Baker, from *The Peregrine*

The eyes of a falcon peregrine weigh approximately one ounce each; they are larger and heavier than human eyes. If our eyes were in the same proportion to our bodies as the peregrine's are to his, a twelve stone man would have eyes three inches across, weighing four pounds. The whole retina of a hawk's eye records a resolution of distant objects that is twice as acute as that of the human retina. Where the lateral and binocular visions focus, there are deep-pitted foveal areas; their numerous cells record a resolution eight times as great as ours. This means that a hawk, endlessly scanning the landscape with small abrupt turns of his head, will pick up any point of movement; by focusing upon it he can immediately make it flare up into larger, clearer view.

- J.A. Baker, from *The Peregrine*

Totem Salmon

by Freeman House

Precocious male chubs arrive first and wait, a wave of reproductive insurance. They are fertile and as ready as any human adolescent, but later the larger males will attempt to exclude them from the final intimacy. The three- and four- and sometimes five-year-old males arrive next, darker and more damaged than their smaller, brighter brothers. They have grown downturned snouts with snaggled teeth. Noses and tails have been abraded white as the heavy fish leaped upstream against rock and waterfall; in some places white fungus grows on the sores. The two age classes avoid each other. None of the fish have eaten since entering fresh water and each individual seems all nerves and attitude. Alternatively edgy and languid, they patrol the pools and the dark spaces beneath the bushes that grow on the banks. Should a larger fish encounter a smaller one, there is a sudden stir: the larger fish will lunge and butt and snap to discipline and chase away the smaller.

The females arrive individually, all purpose and system and sleek intent. Each one of them is searching for a certain configuration of gravel and current that will serve her needs. The gravel must be of a certain size – the size of a small man's fist, say – the water of a depth adequate to float the fish during the work to come. By the time she has traveled this far upstream, there is an imperative apparent in her movements: she is feeling the pressure of the season; timing is all. She ignores predators and works in broad daylight, in bright water.

She powers up against the current over a reach of attractive spawning gravel and drifts back. She powers up again, more slowly now, and seems to inspect the gravel with her nose. She is looking for a place where she will build the nest – the redd – the home of the future of the race. The water is a foot or more deep, with enough velocity and gradient to have carried the smaller cobbles on past. Her muscular tail, strengthened by the long sea journey, abraded and scarred by the struggle upstream, still contains strength enough to move half a yard of gravel, a few cobbles at a time. With the leverage of her whole body behind a turn, a swipe of the tail turns up a rock or two. A cloud of silt drifts downstream and disappears. She turns on her side and slaps the loosed cobbles with her tail – a double-time cadence faster than the palpitating heart of the human witness and loud enough to be heard over the sound of the water, loud enough to be heard by the bears and raccoons that lurk at the river's edge each year at this time. She will dig until there is a depression up to fifteen inches deep in the river's bottom. . . .

As she digs she concentrates on deepening it at the center, building an ovipository, a pocket nest for the protection of her eggs. She may have been at this for hours now, or even days. The male up to this point has shown limited interest. He may drift through the area of activity – especially if another male is showing interest – but he has been of no help in moving rocks. But now the female begins to act like a worker testing the result of her labors to see how close to completion it is. Arching her body, she probes the bottom of the depression with her tail, drifts to the surface of the running water, and probes again.

Once she is satisfied, she hovers

over the redd with her vent over the nest pocket. Her lower jaw drops open; the resistance of the gaping mouth helps her to hold herself in place in the current. While the female has been probing, the male has begun to hover steadily nearby, and he has begun to tremble. Now it seems as if an invisible soupy fog of piscine eroticism rises off the water and envelops the observer. The fog is a dense, cold, quiet mixture of sex, death and inevitability.

A single male will join the female in the nest, quivering now more noticeably. As the two of them turn and turn again to race the length of the redd, the male will frequently cross over the back of the female to swim at her other side; thus the temptation to call the act a "courtship" or "dance." Other males will hover at the periphery of the action. When they come too close, the dominant male makes threatening moves out of the circle toward the intruders. The young jacks turn and flee, but the older, heavier males retreat only slightly, hardly turning out of the way. The tension is thick, palpable.

After a time, some signal passes between the two principals that the female is ready. Side by side, both are now holding their jaws agape to steady themselves against the current. The female's tail is arched down toward the pocket at the bottom of the nest. Both are now trembling with the effort and with the gravity of the moment. The male releases a cloud of milt, milky and sperm-filled. At the same instant, the female releases a portion of her eggs. Often, and nearly faster than the eye can see, one or two other males dash over the scene and add their milt to the mix. For a moment, a milky cloud fills the pool. Another moment and it has washed away downstream. If we are lucky, we will have caught a glimpse of the eggs drifting down, slow comets dimly seen through a dense and fertile fog. Immediately, the female will move upstream of the redd and begin to cover the eggs.

The first few motions of her tail will dislodge no gravel, but will serve to create a current that distributes the eggs more widely between the sheltering interstices of the rocks. Then, with increasing vigor, she will move enough gravel to cover the eggs. The finished nest will be difficult to distinguish from the surrounding bottom of the stream, except that the gravel is cleaner and it may mound up slightly where the eggs are incubating. The nearby depression created in covering the eggs will likely serve as the beginning of the next nest.

Now the process begins again. One of the benefits of carrying thousands of potential embryos is that not all must be risked in a single location. Most female king salmon build three or four redds before they have completed their cycle.

Then silence. The progenitor fish, male and female, will drift to shelter, get caught up against logs or rocks they no longer have the energy to avoid, and begin to die, a process that may take hours or days. Their efforts have left them wounded and raw, and expanses of flesh have been worn away by the female's gravel moving work. The secondary males will move on, perhaps to find other opportunities before their time is up. Females stay to protect their nests against predators until they have no energy left. Eagles, bears, raccoons, and otters have been patrolling the edges of the streams throughout the entire cycle; they feast and feast and feast. In this way a multitude of salmon bodies, carrying nutrients gained thousands of miles away in the depths of the sea, are carried away from the edge of the stream where they will also contribute (and contribute importantly) to the health and fecundity of the forest floor. Those carcasses that decompose in the water will feed microorganisms that will later feed salmonid offspring.

The above is excerpted from **TOTEM SALMON** *by Freeman House.*

The Question

I wake to darkness
wrapped tightly around ponderosa
pines, tangled in the juniper bark,
collected and held in this small valley
by stout cliffs of sandstone.

Above, a sky is born shiny blue.
Dawn licks the underside of
cottony cumulus pink, while I
walk the dark road, deeper
into the forest to ask why
new dawn follows the night with
only the promise of new darkness.

A black crow flying above the
tops of trees, caws the
clouds white, collecting the
remaining dusk in her feathers –
and old matron collecting wild berries
in her apron. And a new sun
held back now by the most delicate
web of pine needles and dew, begins
to fill the forest, abiding only
the darkness of its own shadow.

The day has fully arrived.
In the distance, a squirrel barks and
a Steller's jay chirps loudly from a tree
top at the new sun, as if pleasantly
surprised to find himself and the world
alive this morning.

I walk the sun mottled road to the
cabin, the moment for questions
now passed.

- "Bear," from *Until the Sleeper Speaks*

My artwork is primarily an investigation of Nature and my relationship to her, as well as a search for meaning in something other than myself.

One can view the landscape from the perspective of its watercourses. Though they now require greater effort to approach, they still drain, sculpt and quicken the land creating erosion, sediments, ponds, riffles, and a variety which gives the land its peculiar definition. As an artist it is to these particulars that I must continually return if I am to stay honest and speak of what I have observed and know to be true.

I am convinced that the world is to be found in a grain of sand, or perhaps in a woodlot. However, in southern Michigan the landscape is so thoroughly broken up that one must find solace in the scorned, forgotten places. Here this means the river bottoms, to which I continually return, harboring the wealth of fishes, insects, and plant life I treasure – and I suspect richer in the associated spirit life for being left alone. This is where I go when the need for silence becomes compelling; for, in solitude one can hope to become still enough to discern the subtle voices and begin to perceive the connections. As above, so below; an ancient spiritual principle I accept which makes me a religious artist attempting to portray the face of divinity by drawing upon the physical evidence. I find the evidence most compelling in the silence of the woods. Here lie circuits of living energy,

complex and flexible enough to insure longevity – dynamic equilibria which are eternal. The web of creatures and soil is complete and feeds energy among its layers continuously – nothing wasted, nothing hoarded. Eternal biological and spiritual principles becoming self-evident, recurring in endless variety: branching rivulets, twigs, rootlets, veins, nerves and ideas; life issuing from decay and in its course decomposing; creatures eating and being eaten. Accumulations of excess are merely temporary and self-limiting, wealth being weight. Heartbeats circulate the quickening fluids, like cloudbursts and springs moving the Earth's lifeblood. Water in motion is in truth neither alive nor separable from life, and therein lies its insoluble mystery and inescapable fascination. I suspect that with sufficient attention and familiarity all things cease to be foreign and enter the ranks of the living.

To strive for the center that I am convinced is the locus of a spiritual and therefore sane existence I must look beyond the pain to that which is beautiful, to celebrate the miracle of its existence. Where the miracle is perceived there is hope that its absence will be missed. The danger in treating subject matter about which one cares deeply is that one treads a slippery path between sentiment and sentimentality. Staying safely away from this line of battle, however, makes for anemic art and is ultimately bankrupt.

I spend more time reading, walking, and fishing than drawing. Were I to do otherwise, I would run out of experience and purpose. Thus, my primary teacher is Spirit, mediated by trees and brooks.

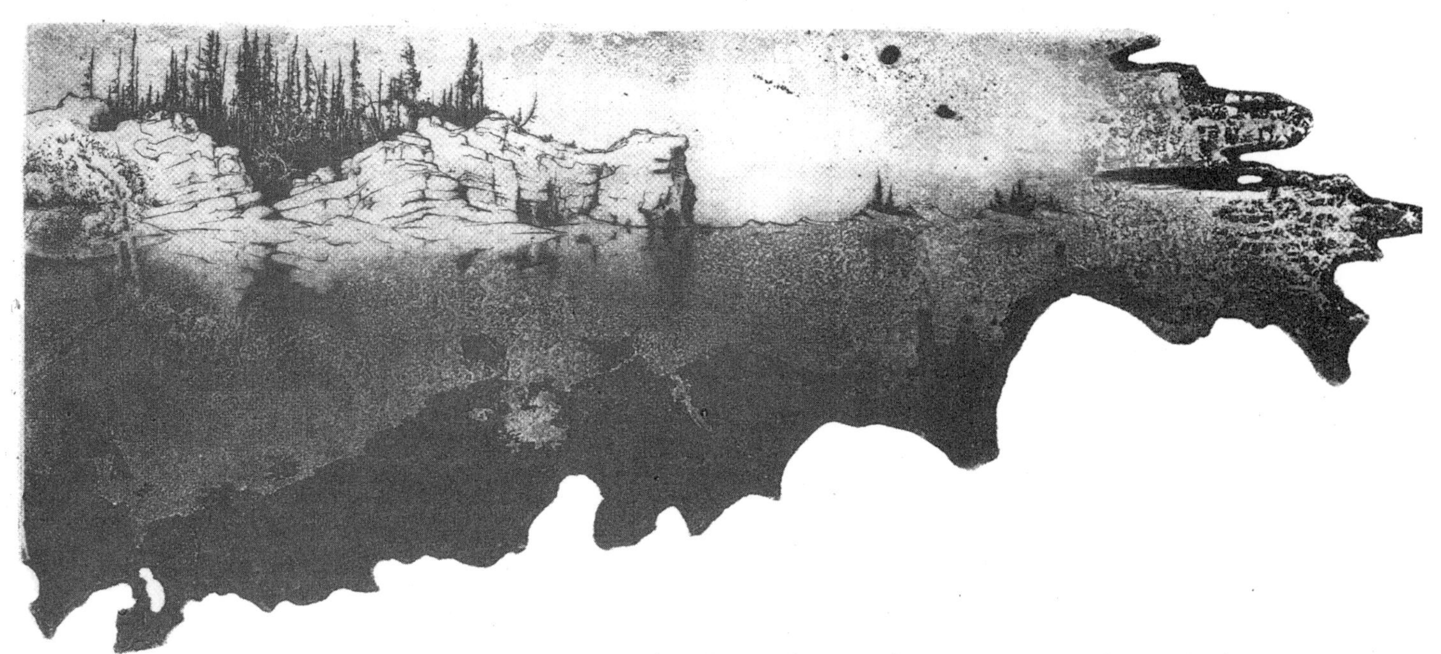

Ladislav Cepelak, a retired professor of printmaking in Prague, works as I think I might at his age were I to stay the course for several decades more – a kindred spirit casting his experiential net across Bach sonatas, winter fields, dismal taverns, chestnut blossoms, moths, Milton, and the craft of violin-making, to come up with a body of work which sings of the full experience of a life lived with both eyes and heart open.

- Ladislav R. Hanka, artist, from the introduction to *50 x 25*, a catalog of a bookbinding exhibit at the Bridwell Library in Dallas, Texas. Mr. Hanka can be reached at 1005 Oakland Drive, Kalamazoo MI 49008.

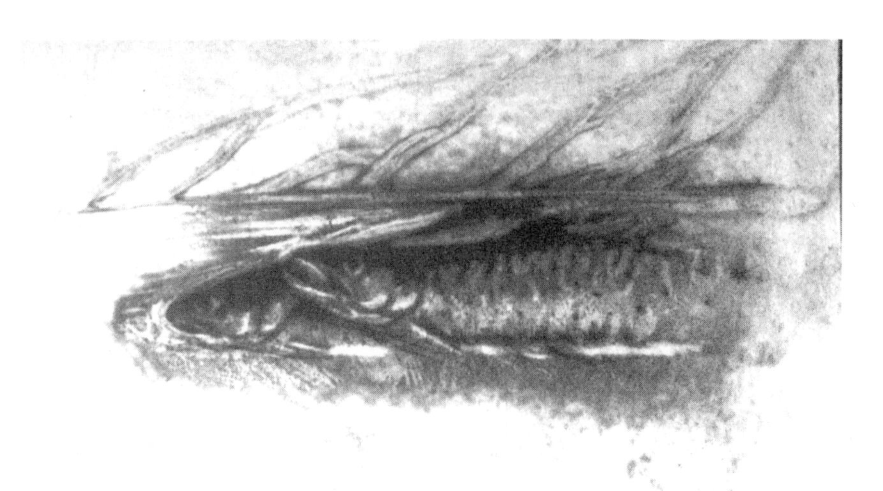

The Legacy of Luna

by Julia Butterfly Hill

Julia Butterfly Hill, activist and author of the book ***The Legacy of Luna*** from which the following excerpt is taken, lived in a giant redwood for 738 days in an effort to save the forest in which it stood from the chainsaws of Pacific Lumber Company. On an otherwise ordinary day, on a car trip with friends in California, Julia experienced this moment that kindled her passion to try to save the redwoods.

- Editor

As I crossed the highway, I felt something calling to me. Upon entering the forest, I started walking faster and faster, and then, feeling this exhilarating energy, I broke into a run, leaping over logs as I plunged in deeper.

After about a half mile, the beauty of my surroundings started to hit me. I slowed down for a better look. The farther I walked the larger the ferns grew, until they were so big that three people with outstretched arms couldn't have encircled them. Lichen, moss, and fungus sprouted everywhere. Around each bend in the path, mushrooms of every shape and size imaginable burst forth in vivid hues of the rainbow. The trees, too, became bigger and bigger. At first they seemed like normal trees, but as I leaned my head back as far as I could, I looked far up into the air. I couldn't even see their crowns. Hundreds of feet high, they were taller than fifteen-, eighteen-, even twenty-story buildings. Their trunks were so large that ten individuals holding hands would barely wrap around them. Some of the trees were hollow, scorched away by lightning strikes, yet they still stood. These trees' ancestors witnessed the dinosaur days. Wrapped in the fog and the moisture they need to grow, these ancient giants stood primordial, eternal. My feet sank into rich earth with each step. I knew I was walking on years upon years of compounded history.

As I headed farther into the forest, I could no longer hear the sounds of the cars or smell their fumes. I breathed in the pure wonderful air. It tasted sweet on my tongue. Everywhere I turned, there was life whether I could see, smell, hear, taste, or touch it or not. For the first time, I really felt what it was like to be alive, to feel the connection of all life and its inherent truth – not the truth that is taught to us by so-called scientists or politicians or other human beings, but the truth that exists within Creation.

The energy hit me in a wave. Gripped by the spirit of the forest, I dropped to my knees and began to sob. I sank my fingers into the layer of duff, which smelled so sweet and so rich and so full of life, then lay my face down and breathed it in. Surrounded by these huge ancient giants, I felt the film covering my senses from the imbalance of our fast-paced, technologically dependent society melt away. I could feel my whole being bursting forth into new life in this majestic cathedral. I sat and cried for a long time. Finally, the tears turned into joy and the joy turned to mirth, and I sat and laughed at the beauty of it all.

Dersu the Trapper

By V. K. Arsen'ev (1872-1930) translated by Malcom Burr

Some books transcend time. They may not be popular when they are first published, but after the bestsellers of the day are long forgotten, ***Sailing Alone Around The World***, ***Moby Dick*** and ***Walden*** are still widely read and talked about.

Dersu the Trapper was written in the 1920s by a Russian army officer about turn-of-the-century travels in remote areas of Siberia. In the forest he meets an Indian, whom he hires as a guide. A deep friendship develops between the two men. Ultimately, over many adventures, each would risk his own life to save the other.

Dersu reminds me of men I have known briefly – people of the land who possessed both inner strength and humility. The notion of the "noble savage" is largely myth – Indians are, and were, of course, capable of all the sins and inadequacies that have shaped human history. And yet, I believe, survival as a hunter/gatherer required a physical and mental strength different from the strength required to succeed in our culture. I suspect that the humility and selflessness that characterized much of their social interaction was born of necessity; to survive they had to develope a set of social skills that enabled them to get along with each other in small groups over long periods of time. The lack of means to store things, whether refrigerators to store food, or money to store human energy, encouraged a slower pace and a more relaxed approach to day-to-day life. A lack of technology and of associated comforts led to humility before the forces of nature. We invent tools to make our lives easier, and then our tools change who we are, our religion and our values.

In 1941, ***Dersu The Trapper*** was translated into English from the Russian by Malcolm Burr. The usage in the book of the "Gold," or "Goldi" is perhaps related to "Mongol." The text also contains references to other cultures that may appear condescending or paternalistic, including words like "Chinamen", that have, for good reason, fallen into disuse. The way these words are used in the book, it seems unlikely that any disrespect was intended.

A few years ago, the Japanese director Kurosawa made a film of the book which he titled ***Dersu Uzala***. Kurosawa's film won an Oscar for best foreign language film for 1975. This led McPherson & Company to publish a new edition of the book in English (the first in 55 years) from which the following excerpt is taken.

Our Nocturnal Visitor

In the year 1902 I was engaged on a survey of the then unmapped country between the rivers Amur and Ussuri on the west and the Sea of Japan on the east, to the north of Vladivostok. It is marked on English maps as the Maritime Province, but is conveniently referred to as Ussuria, from its dominant river. My duties included the making of a reconnaissance of the chief rivers and of the central watershed, the range called Sihote-Alin, which dominates the province. My orders covered the study of the zoology and botany of the district, and of the natives, both aborigines and immigrant. I had with me two assistants and a small detachment of Siberian Rifles and Cossacks, with pack-horses.

It is rough, steep, mountainous country where we were trekking, covered with dense virgin forest, the famous *taiga* of Siberia, in places almost impenetrable, especially where the ground is littered with fallen giants smashed down by storms.

One afternoon, when the sun was low over the horizon, it was time to stop and bivouac. There was an urgent need to find water quickly, for both beasts and men. The slopes were gentle at first, but farther on the gradient became much steeper, and the horses slid down, squatting on their hocks. The packs slipped forward, and if it had not been for the breech-bands they would have fallen over their horses' heads. We were obliged to make long zigzags, and through all the windfalls that littered the ground here it was by no means easy going.

Over the pass we dropped at once into a gulch. The place was extraordinarily broken. Deep screes, encumbered with boulders and trunks, streams and rocks, all thickly overgrown with a carpet of moss; the whole scene reminded me vividly of a picture of Walpurgis Night. It would be hard to imagine a wilder and more repellent scene than that grim gorge.

Sometimes it happens that mountain and forest have such a cheerful and attractive

appearance that one would be glad to linger there forever. In others, mountains seem surly and wild. It is a strange thing that such impressions are not purely personal and subjective, but were felt by all the men in the detachment. I tested this several times and was always convinced that it was so. That was the case here. In that spot there was an oppressive feeling in the air, something unhappy and painful, and the sensation of gloom and ill-omen was felt by us all.

"Never mind," said the rifleman, "we'll manage to bivouac somehow or other. We're not here for a year, and we'll find a jollier place tomorrow."

I did not want to stop there either, but what else could we do? Night was coming on, and there was no time to lose. I could hear the murmur of a brook at the bottom of the defile, so made my way down to it and chose the nearest approach to a level spot and gave orders to pitch camp there.

The silence of the forest was at once broken by the ring of axes and by human voices as the men started collecting firewood, unsaddling the horses, and preparing for supper.

Poor horses! Among those rocks and broken branches they would find little grazing, I feared, but we would make it up for them the next day if we succeeded in getting through to some farmers' cabins.

Darkness comes on early in the forest. In the west a few spots of pale sky were still to be picked out between the black branches of the pines, but below the shades of night had already fallen. As our bonfire sprang into flame, the dark clumps of shrubs and thick trunks of the trees stood out in the glare against the darkness. A little squirrel-like pica, startled among the screes, uttered a high-pitched pipe, but, suddenly frightened, slipped nimbly into its hole and did not appear again.

At length our little party quieted down. After drinking tea, each one of us was busy on his own particular job. One was cleaning his rifle, another repairing a saddle, or darning a piece of torn clothing. There is always plenty of that sort of work to be done. When they had finished, the men turned in to sleep. They pressed up close to each other for warmth, covered themselves with their greatcoats, and slept like the dead. The horses, finding no food among the rocks, came up close to our bivouac, and stood and drowsed. Only Olentiev and I remained awake. I described our road in my diary, and he patched his boots. About ten I rolled myself up in my shaggy Caucasian cloak, or *burka*, and lay down by the fire. The branches of the old fir under which we were

sleeping swayed in the rising column of heat and smoke from the fire, disclosing and closing the dark sky above, all spangled in a long colonnade of stars which faded away gradually into the depths of the forest and imperceptibly merged into the blackness of the night.

Suddenly the horses raised their heads and pricked up their ears, were restive a moment, then quieted down and resumed their drowse. We paid no attention to that and continued our conversation. A minute or two went by. I asked my assistant Olentiev something and, not receiving a reply, turned towards him. He was standing in an attitude of expectancy and, shading the glare of the fire with his hand, gazing into the darkness.

"What's up?" I asked.

"Something coming down the hillside," he whispered.

We both listened, but all around was still, as still as it can be only in the heart of a forest on a cold autumn night. Suddenly some small stones came trickling down from above.

"A bear, I expect," said Olentiev, and began to load his rifle,

"No shoot . . . me man!" came a voice out of the darkness, and a moment later a

man stepped into the light of the fire.

He was dressed in a jacket of deerskin with breeches of the same material. He had a sort of scarf tied round his head and on his feet *unty*, moccasins made of wapiti or elk skin. He had a knapsack of birch bark on his back and in his hands he carried an old rifle, called in Russian a *berdianka*, with *soshki*, or prop, to support it when aiming.

"Morning, captain," he said, greeting me in the way the local tribesmen address all Russians in uniform.

Then he leaned his rifle against a tree, took off his knapsack, wiped the sweat off his face with his sleeve, and sat down by the fire. I had a good look at him.

Our visitor looked about forty-five years of age. He was not very tall, but broad and thickset, and evidently a man of great physical strength. He had a tremendous chest, his arms were strong and muscular, his legs a trifle bowed. His weather-beaten face was typical of the local tribesmen, with his cheekbones, small nose, slanting eyes with the Mongolian fold of the lid, and broad mouth with strong, big teeth. A small reddish mustache edged his upper lip, while his chin was tipped by a short, reddish, skimpy beard. But most remarkable of all were his eyes. These were dark grey rather than hazel, with a calm but somewhat naive expression. Through them there looked out upon the world directness of character, good nature, and decision.

The unknown did not take us in as we did him. From his breast he took out a pouch of tobacco, filled his pipe and started smoking. Without asking him who he was or whence he came, I offered him food. That is the custom in the *taiga*.

"Thanks, captain," he said, "me want eat very much; me not eat all day long."

I watched him while he ate. A hunting-knife hung from his girdle. His hands were gnarled and scarred. Similar, but deeper scars marked his face, one across his brow, another on the neck below the ear. He pulled off his scarf, and I saw that his head was covered with thick, reddish hair, all in disorder, long locks hanging down his neck.

Our guest was taciturn. At length Olentiev could contain himself no longer, and asked him right out:

"Are you a Chinaman or a Korean?"

"Me a Gold," he answered simply.

I was interested to meet one of this disappearing tribe of natives, related to the Manchus and Tungus. I knew there were but about five thousand of them left in Russian territory and a few more in Chinese. They are mostly hunters and fishermen, and such culture as they have is more influenced by China than by Russia, and there are more Buddhists among them than Orthodox, and plenty still are heathen.

"You are, of course, a hunter?" I asked him again.

"Yes," he answered. "Me all time go hunt; no other work; me no can fish, not know; only know hunt."

"And where do you live?" went on Olentiev relentlessly.

"Me no got house; me all time live moving; light fire, make tent, sleep; all time go hunt, how have house?"

He went on to tell us that that day he had been after a wapiti, that he had wounded a doe, but only lightly. Following her spoor, he had come across our tracks, which he had followed down into the gulch. When darkness came on he saw our fire, so came straight to it.

"Me go quiet," he explained, "think what man go far? Go see, captain or Cossack. Me then come straight."

"What's your name?" I then asked the stranger.

"Dersu Uzala," he answered.

This man interested me. There was something unusual and original about him. He spoke simply, quietly, and had a modest, gentle manner. We sat and talked. He told me all about his life, and the more he talked, the more I liked the fellow. Before me I saw a primitive hunter, who had spent his entire life in the *taiga* and was exempt from all the vices which our urban civilization brings in its train. From his words I gathered that everything in life he owed to his rifle, and the results of the chase he gave to the Chinese in exchange for tobacco, lead, and powder, and that his rifle he had inherited from his father. He then told me that he was fifty-three years of age, that he had never had a house in his life, that he had always slept under the open sky and only in winter built himself a hut of bark and brushwood. His first glimmerings of childish memories were of a river, a hut, father, mother, and little sister.

"They all gone dead," he concluded, and became pensive. After a little silence he went on:

"Once me had wife and son and girl child; smallpox kill all; now me alone."

His face became sad at the thought of past suffering. I attempted to offer consolation, but what consolation could I give this lonesome man, whom death had robbed of his family, the only consolation of old age? I felt I wanted to express my sympathy for him, to do something to help him, but I did not know what. Then an idea came to me, and I offered to give him a new rifle in exchange for his old *berdianka*. But he refused, saying that his was an old favorite, that he loved it for the sake of the memory of his father, that he was used to it, and that it killed well. He stretched out his arm to the tree, picked up the old weapon, and began to stroke the stock affectionately.

The stars over our heads had moved on, showing that it was after midnight. The hours sped by, but still we sat over the fire and talked. Dersu did most of the talking, while I sat over the fire and listened, and listened with very real pleasure. He told me about his hunting, and how once he had fallen into an ambush of brigands, and how he had escaped from them. He told me about his encounter with tigers, how he could not shoot them because they are gods who protect ginseng from men; he talked about floods and about evil spirits.

Once a tiger had severely mauled him. His wife tracked him for several days and eventually found him exhausted from loss of blood. While he was ill, she did the hunting.

Then I began asking him about the place where we then were. He told me that it was the source of Lefu and that the next day we should come to the first cabin.

One of the sleeping soldiers awoke, looked in astonishment at us, muttered something to himself, smiled, turned over, and went to sleep again.

On the ground and in the sky it was still dark, but on the side where new stars were rising we could detect the approach of tomorrow. All around, the stillness was impressive. It seemed as through Nature herself was resting.

Another hour, and the east turned crimson. I looked at my watch; it was six o'clock, and time to wake the orderly of the day. I shook him by the shoulder. He sat up and stretched himself. The bright light of the fire dazzled him and he screwed up his eyes. Then, catching sight of Dersu, he smiled and said:

"Hullo. That's rummy, a pal turned up!" and began to pull on his boots.

The sky turned from black to deep blue, and then grey and cloudy. The shades of night began to shrink into the bushes and ravines. In a few minutes our bivouac was astir again; men started talking; the horses stirred at their ropes; a pica piped on one side, and lower down the gorge another answered it; the yaffle of the woodpecker ranged through the forest and the melodious whistle of the oriole. The *taiga* awoke. It grew lighter every moment, and suddenly the dazzling rays of the sun burst out from beyond the mountains and lit up the whole forest. Now our camp had a very different aspect. Instead of the blazing bonfire there lay a pile of ashes, with hardly a glimmer of flame; on the ground there lay the empty tins out of which we had supped; on the spot where my tent had been there stood a naked pole, and the trampled grass.

The Boar Hunt

When we had drunk a mug or two of tea the soldiers began to load up the horses. Dersu also began to make ready. He pulled on his knapsack and picked up his rifle and prop. In a few minutes the detachment was on the road, and Dersu came with us.

The ravine along which we went was long and winding, with similar lateral ravines running into it from the sides, down which mountain streamlets came bustling. The gulch broadened out gradually into a valley. Here the trees had been blazed, which kept us on the trail. The Gold marched ahead, keeping his eye fixed upon the ground. At times he would stoop to pick up a leaf between his fingers.

"What is that?" I asked him.

Dersu stopped and said that the path was not intended for horse traffic, but only for men on foot, that it led to sable traps, and that a man had passed that way some days previously, probably a Chinaman.

The Gold's words surprised us all. Noticing that we looked rather incredulous, he exclaimed:

"How you not know? Look self!"

After this he produced such indications that my doubts were scattered at once. It was all so clear and simple that I was surprised not to have noticed it myself. In the first place there had been no sign of hoof marks, and in the second, none of the twigs on the shrubs bordering the path had been broken off, which would have been the case if horses had been that way, for the trail was narrow for them and the packs kept catching in the branches. The bends were so sharp that horses could not turn round, but were obliged to make little detours, and the tracks across the brooks always led to a tree-trunk bridge, and never into the water; besides, the blown-down branches lying about the track were not broken. All this showed that the trail was not suitable for caravans with pack animals.

"Long time one man he go," continued the Gold as though to himself. "Man he go finish – rain come," and he began to count how many days since the last rain.

For a couple of hours we marched along the trail. Little by little the coniferous forest became mixed and broad-leaved trees more numerous – poplar, maple, aspen, birch, and lime. I wanted to halt but Dersu advised us to go on a little further.

"We soon find hunt," he said, and pointed to some trees from which the bark had been cut.

I understood. It meant that in the neighborhood there must be something for which that bark was wanted. We pushed on and about ten minutes later saw a small hut on the bank of a brook, rigged up by some trapper or ginseng-hunter. Looking round, our new friend repeated that a Chinaman had passed that way a few days previously, and spent a night in the hut. The ashes of his fire, beaten down by the rain, the pile of grass that made his couch, and an abandoned pair of old gaiters of the coarse blue material locally called daba, were clear evidence of that.

I had by now realized that Dersu the Gold was no ordinary man. Before me stood a tracker, and involuntarily my thoughts went back to the delight of my boyhood, Fenimore Cooper and Mayne Reid.

It was time to feed the horses. I decided to take advantage of the opportunity to lie down in the shade of a big cedar, and dropped off to sleep at once. In a couple of hours Olentiev awakened me and I looked around. I saw Dersu splitting firewood and collecting birch bark and stacking it all in the hut.

I thought at first that he wanted to burn it down, and started dissuading him from the idea. Instead of replying he asked me for a pinch of salt and a handful of rice. I was interested to see what he was going to do with it, so told the men to give him some. The Gold carefully rolled up some matches in birch bark, and the salt and rice, each separately, in rolls of birch bark, and hung it all inside the hut. He then started packing his own things.

"You'll probably be coming back here one of these days, I suppose?" I asked him.

He shook his head, so I then asked him for whom he was leaving the matches, salt, and rice.

"Some other man he come," answered

Dersu, "He find dry wood, he find matches, he find food, not die."

I well remember how struck I was by this. It was wonderful, I thought, that the Gold should bother his head about an unknown man whom he never would see, and who would never know who had left him the provisions. I thought how my men, on leaving a bivouac, always burnt up all the bark left at the fire. They did it out of no ill-will, but simply for amusement, to see the blaze, and I never used to stop them from doing so. And here was this savage far more thoughtful for others than I. Why is it that among town-dwellers this forethought for the interests of others has completely disappeared, though no doubt it was once there?

Morning Song

Dawn
rain strikes
elms
Light
gathers
thinly
Raven
sings in the
rain

- Maurice Kenny

Jayber Crow

by Wendell Berry

Of course, I know well what it is to be in a boat in a fog, and mainly I count it among the pleasures. In the early morning in the fog I can't see the river from the porch. I go down the path, following it step by step as it is revealed, and then down the dug steps in the bank to the river's edge. The boat takes shape at first as if it is floating in the air. And then, coming closer, I see its reflection in the water. I loosen the chain and toss it into the boat with a crash that seems more substantial than anything I can see. The fog drifts on a current of air, usually upstream. I step into the boat and feel its buoyancy. Ripples go out from it. I go to the middle seat, place the oars in the locks, and set the boat out onto the water, free of the shore. I row quietly, close along the bank. The river has only the one visible edge. It could be as wide as the ocean. I come to where the end of the trotline is tied to a stout root. I go to the bow seat then and catch the line and raise it. I work my way out along the line from one snooded hook to the next, taking off fish (if any). Now I can see neither shore. The line rises, dripping, out of the water ahead of me and disappears behind. If a fish is on it, I will feel it, something alive out in the fog, down in the dark. Sometimes, after being bent to my work for a while, I will straighten up and see that the fog has lifted and I am again in the known world.

Back at the house, with the river and its mood still in my mind, I fix breakfast and (if the weather is fine) eat out on the porch. And then I have my shave and set the place to rights. If the fog has cleared, the sunlight, glancing off the river, will be rippling and swaying on the walls and ceiling of my house, so that for a while I seem to be living within the element of living light.

If the mosquitoes will leave me alone, I love to sit or lie out on the porch and watch the dark come. Past sundown, the light is charmed, the way it is in the early morning. First there will be the swallows circling and dipping over the river. Maybe a kingfisher will come rattling by, skimming close above the surface of the water. Maybe I will see herons flying to roost. And then the bats begin to flicker in and out of sight, and the fireflies rise up out of the weeds, lighting their little lights, and the

stars come out. Past a certain time, the darkness and quietness are present all around, the night creatures begin their calls, and you can feel something of the inward life of the world.

In the late winter the owls begin to mate and I hear the paired ones calling to each other, back and forth. The wood ducks begin to pair off. I see them sitting together in the trees near the house, and hear the hen ducks crying as they fly. I know spring is coming when, one morning, I hear a phoebe calling, and the woodpeckers drum on hollow trees and the tin roof of my house. Spring has certainly come when I hear the little yellow-throated warbler that sings in the tops of the tallest sycamores. In the summer dusk there is always a peewee calling his name from a dead branch somewhere on the edge of an opening. The Carolina wren sings the whole year round. I hear the frogs and toads at night, starting with the peepers in early spring, and later the crickets and katydids. Something wild is always blooming, from twinleaf and bloodroot early in spring to beeweed in late fall, things of intricate, timeless beauty. Often I fear that I am not paying enough attention.

And how many hours have I spent in watching the reflections on the water? When the air is still, then so is the surface of the river. Then it holds a perfectly silent image of the world that seems not to exist in this world. Where, I have asked myself, *is* this reflection? It is not on the top of the water, for if there is a little current the river can slide frictionlessly and freely beneath the reflection and the reflection does not move. Nor can you think of it as resting on the bottom of the air. The reflection itself seems a plane of no substance, neither water nor air. It rests, I think, upon quietness. Things may rise from the water or fall from the air, and, without touching the reflection, break it. It disappears. Without going anywhere, it disappears.

Here on the river I have known peace and beauty such as I never knew in any other place. There is always work here that I need to be doing and I have many worries, for life *on* the edge seems always threatening to go *over* the edge. But I am always surprised, when I look back on times here that I know to have been laborious or worrisome or sad, to discover that they were never out of the presence of peace and beauty, for here I have been always in the world itself.

Black Marsh Ecologue

Although it is midsummer, the great blue heron
holds darkest winter in its hunched shoulders,
those blue-burning-grey clouds
rising over him like a storm from the Pacific.

He stands in the black marsh,
more monument than bird, a wizened prophet
returned from a vanished mythology
He watches the hearts of things

and does not move or speak. But when
at last he flies, his great wings
cover the darkening sky, and slowly,
as though praying, he lifts, almost motionless,

as he pushes the world away.
- Sam Hamill

From the book ***Destination Zero: Poems 1970-1985*** published
by White Pine Press, reprinted here by permission of Sam Hamill.

Atchafalaya Autumn

by Greg Guirard

Lake Fausse Pointe – North Shore
Nighttime – January 4, 1994

My plan is to come here every week for three days and nights and do photography and writing for my new book. I've been working on the photography and the writing for years, but this is my first day and night at Lake Fausse Pointe, and I wanted very badly to catch the sunset. Time was running out, so I took off from my house at 4:10 PM in my '79 Cadillac. I had a blowout about five miles down the levee, changed the tire in exactly five minutes. Next I noticed steam coming from under the hood – broken water hose. Fixed it temporarily and headed on to Roy Blanchard's house where I had left one of my boats in the water behind his house. The boat had been pushed up on some rocks and cypress knees by a strong north wind. Then the water dropped, leaving the boat stranded. With superhuman determination I muscled it back into the water and loaded everything into it – gasoline and oil, bedding, food, battery for lights, cameras, propane stove, more food, flannel sheets, you-name-it. Finally I got out on the water, with the sun close to setting. The sunset at

Lake Fausse Pointe, shot from behind big cypress trees, was fine. A golden glow stayed in the sky for half an hour after sunset. When all the light was gone, I went to my houseboat and ate: crawfish étouffée cornbread, salad of cabbage, carrots, apples, raisins, pineapples. Then I sat here to write: My propane stove is blazing away.

It's very quiet and peaceful here, no boats, no dogs barking, no frogs croaking, no automobile sounds, nothing but tiny waves lapping on the side of the boat, the sound of my stove, and some gurgling among the cypress knees and tree trunks. I'm getting there, Henry David.

I feel very good about this venture, this time I will spend trying to make a book that is very personal, and trying to slow down so that I can enjoy being myself and doing what I do. Today was a beautiful beginning, though it seemed I was destined to get out here too late. The evening light was magic. The trees seemed to glow. Far out across the lake, more than two miles from the houseboat, I could see a large flock of white pelicans, and they glowed too, with a kind of golden-pink color. I have a strong feeling that there is no one within miles of where I sit. And that is fine with me.

Excerpted from ***ATCHAFALAYA AUTUMN***. For order information, please see page 72.

In A Country of Light, Among Animals

By Barry Lopez, excerpted from the book **About This Life**

I don't know, of course, whether you've ever been in the high Arctic in summer, but I would begin by telling you how striking the light is. For two months or more the sun doesn't dip below the horizon. In a treeless, winter-hammered landscape like Alaska's north slope, the light creates a feeling of compassion that is almost palpable. Each minute of light experienced feels like one stolen from a crushing winter. You walk gently about, respectful of flowering plants, with a sense of how your body breaks the sunshine, creating a shadow. You converse in soft tones. The light is – perhaps there is no other word – precious. You are careful around it.

The wind always feels close here, a gentle breeze, a heavy blow, the breathing of an unfathomable welter of clouds which passes continually overhead, an ocean in which weather is being conceived. It's figuring out what it wants to do before moving south and east across North America: now altostratus, now cirrus, now cumulonimbus, like exercises. After lunch a mare's tail sky; at one in the morning a rainbow appears to the south, half as broad as my fist, driven into the tundra like a sheet of iridescent steel.

But for the wind against your ear and the keening of fifty species of birds, it is as quiet as the moon. The wind surrounds the bark of a fox and it evaporates. In sun-warmed, goose-down clothing, you turn your cheek to the source of light and feel sheltered; you see amid the dwarf birch and dwarf willow at your feet speckled eggs cradled in birds' nests. The grace so apparent in first life seems nowhere else so tender, because night never comes here.

From the slope of a hill above this river, you can look out across two hundred square miles of tundra through air transparent as a polished windowpane. If the Earth were flat, you could see all the way to Iowa. It was into the expansive country, this place of interminable light and clear, rolling air, that Bob and I had come. In it we would watch wolves.

. . .At 2:30 one morning Bob rose to look through his scope and spotted a grizzly bear at the wolf den. A yearling male, the lone sentinel with the pups, charged immediately and drove it back down the cutbank. Even at this distance we could see the puffs of dust at their feet as they raced down the incline. Suddenly the bear spun around and chased the wolf, but only about twenty-five feet before they faced off. Motionless, they stared at each other for a few seconds; then the wolf turned his back and walked away. The bear, now some four hundred feet from the den entrance, his curiosity piqued, walked around to the north and stood up on his hind legs, looking around, sniffing. The young wolf eyed him. The bear quartered back slowly toward the den and then charged. The wolf ran to meet him. Both stopped short, staring. In a few moments the wolf turned around and walked calmly back to the den. The bear ambled down to the creek and disappeared into the willows. The wolf weighed perhaps eighty pounds; the bear weighed three to four hundred pounds and appeared to Bob to be a young boar.

The wolf spent the next fifteen minutes with his nose to the ground, retracing all the bear's movements before finally lying down to sleep.

. . . Four and a half hours after the yearling wolf drove the bear off, about seven in the morning, we saw an adult female wolf traveling toward the den at a steady trot, a laminar flow over the contours of the land. The slight discoloration of hair around her mammae, her round-as-a-melon belly, and her overall bearing revealed – to the Nunamiut, who taught Bob, who showed me – who she was (mother), where she'd been (successfully hunting), and where she was going (home). She stopped briefly a quarter mile west of her current den at a new den site the wolves had been excavating, and then continued on. She came to a sudden dead halt at a spot where the bear's still fresh trail crossed hers. She investigated it for a few moments before going on quickly to the den. The pups charged up out of the ground to greet her, jumping and pawing and bowling one another over in their efforts, seemingly, to embrace. She regurgitated meat for them and the yearling. After nursing the pups, she sniffed all around the den area and curled up to sleep.

An hour and a half later she roused her pups and headed west with all of them trailing clumsily after her. She led them to the new den, a move, we speculated, precipitated by the bear.

Several years ago, at roughly the time *Heron*
Dance was conceived, I interviewed Len Soucy at The Raptor Trust outside Millington, New Jersey. Thirty years ago, Len, who was then a tool and die cutter, and his wife Diane, started to care for injured birds. Over the years, this work gradually took over their lives and several acres of their back yard. Now, dozens of large bird cages temporarily house the thousands of injured birds that are brought to them each year by area residents or sent to them from all over North America. The Raptor Trust also has a few permanent internees that are used in the Raptor Trust's educational program – eagles, hawks, owls and falcons that have imprinted on humans or that have injuries that prevent them from being reintroduced to the wild.

During the interview, I asked Len what he thinks about at night when he walks alone among the cages, feeding the owls. As he walks, wild owls in the trees outside the cages can often be heard calling to the incarcerates.

I think about what a truly marvelous world we inhabit. A really, really interesting, diverse, marvelous place to have visited for a short time. Some get more out of it than others. Some of us try to get more out of it than others. . . .I think you should make a conscientious effort to try. To be nosy. To look and to marvel. And not only to look but to see. Not only listen but hear on all different levels. It is indeed a marvelous world. Part of what makes it marvelous is our own kind. Part of what makes it incredibly marvelous to me are other than our own kind. I think it is important biologically to have them, but it's also important for my quality of life. I would not want to live in a world that had only people in it. I like snakes and frogs and creepy, crawly things and marvelous birds that can fly two hundred miles an hour and free my spirit. . . .

- Len Soucy, "Bird Man of the Great Swamp", From HERON DANCE, Issue 1

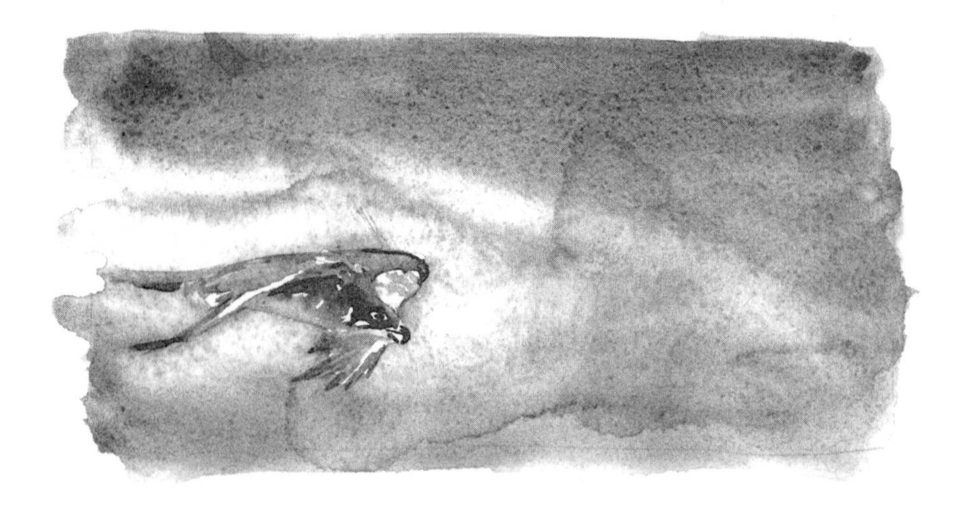

At half past ten, clouds of small birds sprayed up from the fields and a merlin cleaved through them like an arrow, dipping and darting. It was a thin narrow falcon, flying low. It swept over the sea-wall, curved out across the saltings, and swung up into steep spirals, its long sting-like body sawing in the blur of its jabbing, flicking wings. It flew fast, yet its wide circling seemed laborious and its rising slow. At three hundred feet it came round in a long curve, and poised, half-hovering. Then it flew forward into the wind towards a skylark singing high above the fields. It had seen the lark go up, and had circled to gain height before making an attack. From behind, the merlin's wings looked very straight. They seemed to move up and down with a shallow, flicking action, a febrile pulsation, much faster than any other falcon's. It reached the lark in a few seconds, and they fell away towards the west, jerking and twisting together, the lark still singing. It looked like a swallow chasing a bee. They rushed down the sky in zigzags and I lost them in the green of distant fields.

Their rapid, shifting, dancing motion had been so deft and graceful that it was difficult to believe that hunger was the cause of it and death the end. The killing that follows the hunting flight of hawks comes with a shocking force, as though the hawk had suddenly gone mad and had killed the thing it loved. The striving of birds to kill, or to save themselves from death, is beautiful to see. The greater the beauty the more terrible the death.

- J.A. Baker, from *The Peregrine*

Woodpigeons and jackdaws went up from North Wood at midday, and cawing crows flew to their treetop stations. Chaffinches by the bridge scolded steadily for ten minutes, their monotonous 'pink, pink' gradually dying away in the sunlit silence. I saw nothing. Assuming the hawk to have soared down wind, I searched for him north of the ford and found him in the dead oak half an hour later. He flew up into the wind and began to circle. His wingbeats became shallower, till only the tips of his wings were faintly fluttering. I thought he would soar, but instead he flew quickly southeast. The line that divides North Wood dips and rises through a steep-sided gully, which is sheltered from the wind. The peregrine has learned that warm air rises from the sunny, windless slopes of the lane, and he often flies there when he wishes to soar.

Slowly he drifted above the orchard skyline and circled down wind, curving upward and round in long steep glides. He passed from the cold white sky of the south, up to the warm blue zenith, ascending the wind-bent thermal with wonderful ease and skill. His long-winged, blunt-headed shape contracted, dwindled, and darkened to the flinty point of a diamond as he circled high and far over; hanging and drifting above; indolent, watchful, supreme. Looking down, the hawk saw the big orchard beneath him shrink into dark twiggy lines and green strips; saw the dark woods closing together and reaching out across the hills; saw the green and white fields turning to brown; saw the silver line of the brook, and the coiled river uncoiling; saw the horizon staining with distant towns; saw the estuary lifting up its blue and silver mouth, tongued with green islands. And beyond, beyond all, he saw the straight-ruled shine of the sea floating like a rim of mercury on the surface of the brown and white land. The sea, rising as he rose, lifted its blazing storm of light, and thundered freedom to the landlocked hawk.

- J.A. Baker, from *The Peregrine*

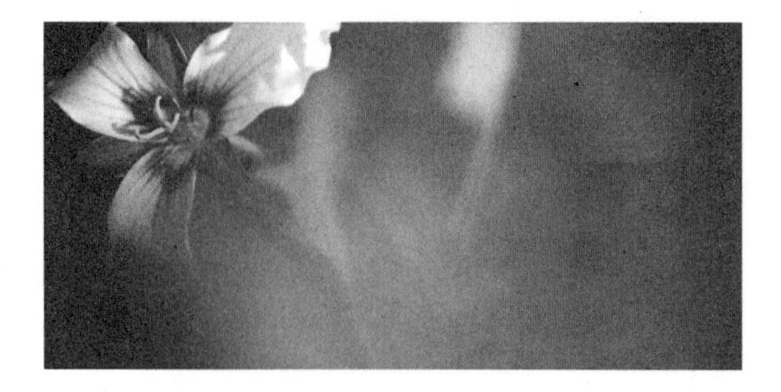

Natural Causes

by Walt McLaughlin

For thousands of years philosophers have speculated about what is real, as if reason could do what the five senses cannot. The discussion almost always goes astray, sinking deep into the quagmire of semantics until it all seems like so much frivolous wordplay. But life itself takes center stage in any heartfelt consideration of the matter. And death, of course, is right there with it. Such discussions usually occur indoors, in urban areas, in halls of higher learning where books and papers are the fundamental reality. Yet deep in the nearby forest an unending drama is being played out with all the intensity of creation and apocalypse, undercutting the petty abstractions of the frail human mind. Oddly enough, philosophers like me retreat into the forest to relax, to escape the heaviness of abstract thoughts and simply be in the world for a while. We do not expect to learn anything in the process.

The surrounding trees slowly take shape in the first light of day as I crawl from underneath my tarp. Jesse, a long-haired German Shepherd and faithful companion, follows my lead. She emerges from the same makeshift shelter to yawn, stretch and relieve herself. A quick breakfast, then we bushwhack back to the trail a hundred yards away, leaving our camp hidden in the thick brush along Bourn Brook. The trail is shrouded with mist.

Fly rod in hand, I set a brisk pace while moving northward up the trail. Jesse lags behind, temporarily distracted by some irresistible smell. A moment later she bounds ahead of me. For a half hour we travel like that, winding deeper into Vermont's Lye Brook Wilderness. Eventually, a slight elevation change queues me to the small wetland that I'm using as a navigational landmark. I leave the trail, following a compass bearing due east beyond the wetland. Winhall River is a half mile ahead, snaking along the easternmost boundary of the wilderness area. The descent to it is steep so Jesse and I choose our footing carefully. Less than an hour from camp, we reach the fast-moving amber stream. I pause just long enough on the bank to assemble my fishing gear before stepping into the cool water.

As any seasoned flyfisher will tell you, timing is everything. Last night I enjoyed a busy hour just before dusk, extracting a half dozen small trout from Bourn Brook despite the lingering midsummer heat. This morning I expect even better action. Bigger trout should rise from this substantially larger stream before the sun burns away the thin mist and heats the water enough to stop the ongoing fly hatch. I thread the leader though the guides of my rod with expectant joy. Jesse wades up to her chest in the nearest pool and drinks her fill before breaking into a toothy, water-dripping smile.

A raven calls in the distance – a sure sign that we are in a wild place. The constant rush of clear water over stones soothes the ear. The leaves of birch trees hanging over the stream barely rustle in a faint breath of air. Already yesterday's sweaty, eight-mile trek has been justified by the prevailing forest silence. A slight sprinkle from an overcast sky darkens the stones at my feet, deepening the emerald gleam of the mossy stream bank. A squadron of black flies attacks me while I'm tying a dry fly to my leader but I don't mind too much. The stream dances before me, its cascading water smelling of ozone, and I am free at last from my own stuffy thoughts.

Fecundity is the first law of nature, or so it seems as one meanders through the northern forest. Life is abundant and cheap. Beneath a canopy of leaves thick enough to screen out most daylight, there's a tangle of hobblebush, striped maple and other woody shrubs. Young, slow-growing conifers conspire with the rotting carcasses of fallen trees to make bushwhacking slow and difficult. The forest floor itself is a mosaic of ferns, mosses, lichens and a hundred different flowering plants. There are mushrooms on fallen limbs, chipmunks rummaging amid dead leaves, worms twisting through raw earth and airborne insects everywhere. The natural world is an endless riot of living and dying things, of biomass so thick that there seems no end to it. The swampy, stagnant pools are covered with algae. Fungus grows on every boulder. It is impossible to escape the dank smell of life and death intermingling.

What is real? A deep woods wanderer doesn't bother asking that question. It takes all of one's energy just to keep pace with the highly animated forest. Leave such questions to those who can ponder them in the relative sterility of quiet rooms. This isn't the time or place for idle speculation.

After a full hour of casting, I begin wondering what's wrong. I snatch a mayfly from the air, then match it with one of my artificials. Still no luck. A hundred casts and only one halfhearted rise. Jesse spooks a trout waiting patiently for breakfast in the middle of a pool. Its dark silhouette flashes across the shallow water for an instant before disappearing beneath a half-submerged rock. I spook another one a few minutes later. The fish are here; they just aren't rising. The windless air is thick with wet heat already. Maybe that's the problem. No matter. I keep moving and casting, moving and casting....I'm happy enough simply walking this stream, enjoying the interplay of stone and water at every turn.

But the forest is full of surprises. Just when I have resigned myself to an uneventful morning, I spot something atop a boulder about thirty yards ahead. It seems strangely out of context. Jesse also sees it so I tell her to stay behind me as we approach. Slowly it comes into focus: a rather large bird lying belly down on the gray rock, wings spread apart and face cocked to one side. It's a kingfisher – a fully matured male as big as a woodpecker. It must be dead, I tell myself, but its eyes open halfway when I prod it with a stick. Then they flutter and close. The kingfisher's beak opens and shuts repeatedly, as if the old bird is trying to tell me something. Suddenly I feel uneasy, like a

voyeur caught in the act. So I toss the stick aside and step away.

Despite my self-consciousness, I succumb to curiosity. I go back to the dying bird and carefully inspect it. The kingfisher's plumage has a healthy luster. There is no injury – no blood, loose feathers or broken bones. From all outward appearances, the kingfisher is fine. Mind boggling. I have seen much carnage in the wild. I have witnessed the messy demise of many forest creatures over the years but never anything like this.

Jesse doesn't even try to figure it out. She simply sees the bird for what it is – a golden opportunity. Jesse creeps in closer, hoping that I'll let her take full advantage of the situation. "No!" I shout at her so she recoils. Then I command her to stay at my side as I gradually draw away from the dying creature. Jesse obeys under protest, emitting a low-pitched groan.

About fifty yards from the kingfisher, I sit down on a rock. From this vantage point the bird is only a tiny blue speck resting motionless on a boulder. I start thinking about an older generation, about relatives living and dead, about my parents – my father in particular. His most recent heart attack has made it clear to me that he won't be around forever. There's absolutely nothing that I can do about it, either. I am a mere observer gazing through the window of time at unalterable events. It is easy to ask, "What is real?" but hard to face up to reality. Life runs its course. Death is final. These simple facts hit me with such force that I can't help but shed a few tears. I am overwhelmed by the starkness of it all, by the horror of unbending truth. Only then does it dawn on me that I've never seen a wild creature die of natural causes. Not until now.

I turn to my faithful companion while wiping away the tears but she's not there. Instead Jesse has crept halfway back to the kingfisher with all the stealth of a bonafide predator. Once again I shout "No!" after her. She veers away from the object of her attention, skulking into the dark shadows of the forest. Jesse knows that I mean business but there is something else driving her, something that runs deeper than the bond between us. A few yards downstream of the kingfisher, she emerges from the forest. Silhouetted in a sudden blaze of morning light, Jesse looks more wolfish and menacing than I've ever seen her look before. So I get up and walk back to the bird as if to claim it. Jesse relents and the contest is over, just like that. We continue upstream, around the bend and out of sight – a fly rod whipping the air and a canine looking for brand new opportunities.

One more hour of practice casting then I quit the stream. Jesse stays closeby as we bushwhack through a dense stand of spruce on a shortcut back to the trail. We play together in a forest clearing to partially erase from memory that incident on the stream. Then we return to our camp along Bourn Brook. Later on I gather up my things and move south to Bourn Pond where the fecundity of the forest gives way to open water, air and light. There we are greeted by a loon. Its cry echoes across the pond as if to assure me that I've made the right decision.

Natural causes? It is no more practical to dissect that term than it is to ponder reality. The wild has its way of rendering such notions absurd, of making it clear that the world cannot be grasped by reason alone. So I fix dinner for Jesse and myself from the dried provisions I've brought with me, quite satisfied to forego the taste of fresh fish. Then we sit together by the pond at dusk – a philosopher and his dog watching trout rise and mosquitoes buzz as the last threads of light fade away. The loon swims about nonchalantly, occasionally diving for its dinner. An owl hooting in the distance keeps me from drifting too far into my abstractions. And life is good.

NATURAL CAUSES was originally published as a 3" by 5" pocketbook. For information on this and other books of fine nature writing by Walt and authors selected by Walt, contact Wood Thrush Books, 85 Aldis Street, St. Albans, VT 05478 email: wtbooks@sover.net.

Trees dance
Even on the stillest days.
The dance forms
In the upward arc of the trunk
And explodes
As the canopy catapults
Into the sunlight.

Function cannot
Abide the spontaneity
Of the dance.
The tree is milled,
Its dance buried
Beneath planes and right angles.

I work the milled cube with mallet and gouge
Feeling for the dance.

Sometimes the dance favors the bowl.

Sometimes it is lost.

- Kees Wagenvoord

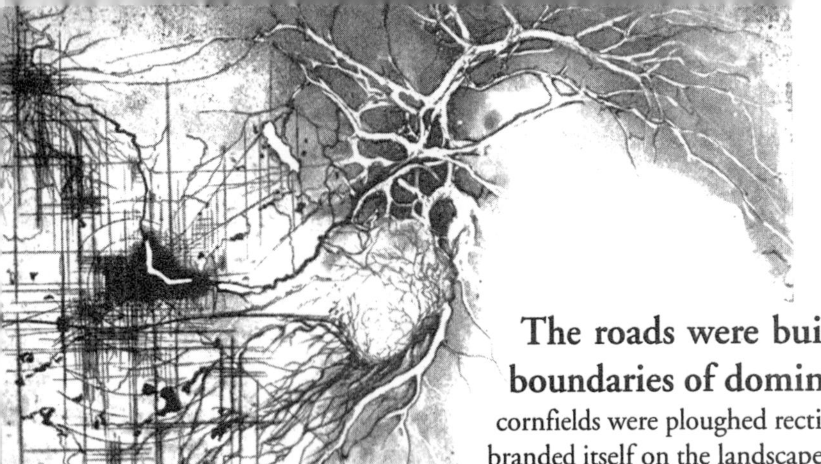

The roads were built at right angles, respecting boundaries of dominion, and the wheat and cornfields were ploughed rectilinear as Euclidean exercises. The map branded itself on the landscape, and an arbitrary portion of the earth became Kalamazoo County.

Yet even 150 years later, the map does not equal the land. Though the county map shows only roads, in the white spaces between them the whole complicated nexus of life, though altered from presettlement wilderness, still pulses. It includes all the commerce we are unaware of, the cycles of growth and decay, the movement of water and air and sunlight, the pathways of animals and the flightpaths of birds. Few of us are aware of this complexity in our landscape. More precise maps are available – U.S. Geological Survey maps will acquaint us with the sensuous contours of hill and valley; the state hydrological maps show us the secret flow of groundwater under our feet. But where is the map that shows us the shadows on the fields, or the high currents of air above us?

Our abstract, post-Enlightenment turn of mind seeks to abandon all uncertainties, all subtleties for the glories of general law. Faced with the variety of nature, we must quantify it, subdue it to the principles of science, shrink it to legal diagram and equation – otherwise it sings too loudly of an order more complex than our own, one less flattering to our sense of mastery. How much more comfortable we are in our houses, among the symbols of our society which tell us we are powerful, we are immortal. At the edge of the forest, we are neither immortal nor privileged. We are a link in the carbon chain.

- James Armstrong from an essay entitled "County Maps" in the publication ***County Survey***, with thanks to Ladislav R. Hanka.

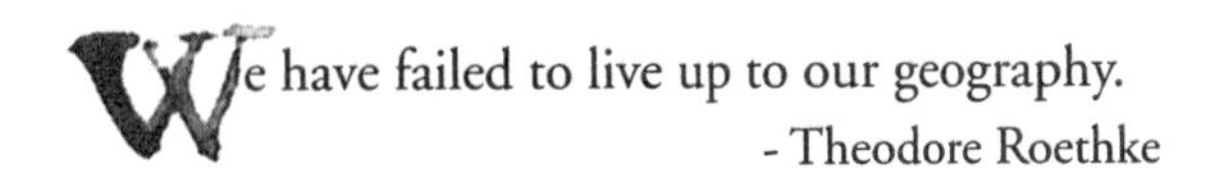

We have failed to live up to our geography.

- Theodore Roethke

Living Inside Hope

by Ann O'Shaughnessy

Last week my older sister wrote in a letter to me: "Sometimes I get lost in your wake. But I have learned to trust this. That is all I have to say." This came at a time I was feeling lost myself. I had hiked the night before to the top of Snake Mountain. The warm wind blew fiercely, grabbing away the words I was muttering to myself. I found a place where the rocks at the edge of the summit made a small hollow and curled up there facing the wind. I was waiting for faith to return. I wanted to feel the familiar warmth and light that spreads inside whenever I let my raw-self open up to the sky. But it did not happen and I walked down in the dark disappointed.

Barbara Kingsolver wrote: "The very best you can do in your life is to figure out what you hope for. And the most you can do is live inside that hope…not admire it from the distance, but live right in it, under its roof." My mother included these words in a letter to me years ago when I had no idea what it meant to live inside your hope. At that time, I had so carefully padded myself from my heart and soul's hoped-for life that I could only look at living that way as an irresponsible frivolity – a dreamer's way.

Somewhere along the way I had come to believe that committing yourself to your dream was not for someone like me, but was the exclusive territory of poets and artists, eccentrics and brilliant outcasts. So I hung onto someone else's borrowed dream, tried my damnedest to live rationally, until the day my soul rebelled and the game was up. Saying good-bye to my life, as I knew it for ten years, took courage. I had nothing: no job, no place to live, and few supporters. Yes, there was an exhilaration around those changes that fueled me. I felt like I was finally on the hero's journey. The joy of finally honoring my truth buoyed me. But living with integrity, I discovered, requires courage far beyond what it takes to make those initial changes. Keeping myself clear of self-doubt, guilt, and fear is still the order of nearly every day. We are all taught early on to step in line, to not complain, to make do – it is radical to refuse, and ultimately it is isolating. Very little in school teaches us how to live sanely outside the lines. My friend JoAnna said to me, "To live truthfully is to open the aperture and look deeper and deeper into yourself, for your true self. And, you know what, there is no dogma, no religion, no creed to support what you find; nothing saying that what you find is worth risking everything for. There is little company on this path. And when your courage fails, you doubt the entire journey."

I have known the bliss of honoring my truth – the feeling of rightness and faith and flow. But I did not predict what I felt up there: isolation, nakedness, hopelessness, and a longing for affirmation. Coming home through the dark, I could only feel my way by my feet on the trail and by looking up for the path outlined by the dark of the sky against the darker treetops. I stopped often to smell and listen. Wood thrush, peepers, grasshoppers. At the end of the hike down, there are a hundred yards of dense woods between the main trail and our house. As I step into these woods, I lose the guidance of the gap in the canopy above and can only discern faint outlines of trees and branches ahead of me. I know that I will sooner or later stumble through far enough to be guided by the lights of the house, but for a while I become completely submerged in the darkness. Groping with my hands outstretched I let myself feel "lost." There is a small panicky feeling, but after ten minutes I stop trying so hard to "see," and soon the lights of our home appear.

I cannot say that all that I felt up on the mountain disappeared as I curled up in my bed that night, but I can say that I let go of the fear. And thinking of my sister's words, I too began to trust the feeling of being lost in my wake.

In the moments before sleep, my thoughts, strangely enough, traveled to a simple little book I read back in February called *Mary's Way: A Memoir of the Life of Mary Cooper Back.* I have thought of this book more and more often lately. A subscriber, Ruth Lamb compiled this memoir from Mary's letters and journals after Mary's death in 1991. Ruth's narration of her aunt's life is plainly written and Mary's own writing often sentimental, but I found myself relishing this book. Meditating on her life before I fell asleep, I began to feel faith and courage seep back into my veins.

I think JoAnna is right. There *is* little company on this path, but I think that when it does come, it fills us deeply. Initially, Mary's life inspired me on a practical level: If she can follow her dream so can I. Here was the role model I did not know I had been searching for: a woman who was both intellectually curious and emotionally tender; a daring adventurer who stayed hungry throughout her life for what moved her, yet who committed herself to love and service. What sustained her life was a connection with nature, art and a deep faith in the interrelatedness of all things. Rarely a day went by when she did not stop, open up and take in the beauty around her. Yet, she was a pragmatist – a scrappy survivor, not a philosophical dreamer. Her words reflect an enduring youthful spirit. What I was now discovering, three months after reading it, was that Mary's book was effecting me in a deeper way. It is hard to find words to describe this impact. It is not a spiritual handbook, nor is it the memoir of the life of a great spiritual leader, but for me the story is deeply spiritual. It is a story of a real life filled with real world problems – not of a monk's epiphanies voiced from his solitude.

Snowy Egret by Mary Back

Mary had a vision for her life that she shared with her husband, Joe Back, whom she met at the Art Institute of Chicago. They wanted to live amidst the "wild valleys and mountains of Wyoming" and to live as artists. They stuck to that dream with tenacity and their story is amazing to witness. During her lifetime Mary was a taxidermist, a naturalist, a schoolteacher, a librarian, a dude rancher, a homesteader, an airplane engine mechanic and a lay minister. She was a proficient hunter, a skilled horsewoman, an able carpenter, and a nurse to many sick or injured creatures. She founded the Wind River Valley Artist Guild, which is now partially supported by her and Joe's estate. The list of their travails and adventures is too long to mention here, but what astounded me and continues to stay with me is their tenacity, creativity and passion for living. Yet they were humble, gentle, giving people – full of love and humor. After struggling for many years to support their work as authors and artists, Joe and Mary eventually found a degree of success and recognition creating bronze figures depicting the American West, and by writing and painting. They lived inside their hope daily – they lived "right in it, under its roof."

When I finished reading the book, I wanted to meet and talk with the author, Ruth Lamb. I looked at the book jacket and discovered that she lived within two hours. I contacted her and asked for an interview. She responded with a heartfelt, "Yes! Come on over" and then some practical advice: "You'll have to come over soon or wait 'til late May when our road dries up. I'd hate for you to get stuck in the mud." It was all I needed to get in my car and travel the two hours to their remote home in east central New York. There were questions that I wanted to ask, but mostly I wanted to witness the influence of Mary Cooper Back on her niece's life. And in her way and words I saw it. I saw the suppleness that comes from daring to change your course and the courage and faith to sustain it. Twelve years ago, at ages 55 and 56, Ruth and her husband Sandy, gave up their comfortable life near Boston to move into the 1860 farmhouse that they had just inherited. They told me they moved when the death from AIDS of a young friend forced them to reexamine what really mattered in life.

Sandy and Ruth's small house is at the end of a three-mile dirt road in the Adirondacks. There is no electricity, no phone and only one cold water tap. Their house is heated by a single cookstove in the kitchen, which also warms the water for the small bathtub that sits in the corner. Above their door is the sign: "Journey's End." Indeed, I felt I had come to the end of a long journey; it had been many months since I had traveled to different woods. As I got out of my car I was stunned by the bird song. Loud and raucous and sweet – purple finches and evening grosbeaks dominated the feeders and trees. What a welcome after such a long winter. (Ruth and Sandy assist the Cornell Ornithology Lab by counting birds in their area.) Walking in, I was promptly greeted by two warm faces and fed hot soup and warm bread.

I asked Ruth, "How has living here these past twelve years affected you?" Her answer was simple: "We notice things more. We live in the present moment more." Sandy Back added, "When you slow down and pay attention it is amazing how much more you see. Mary had this ability." No matter where Mary was, she uncovered beauty in her surroundings. Several times in her life she had to live in urban areas, seemingly cut off from the wild nature she loved. During her time in Chicago she wrote:

> The lake is up tonight. Last night when I came down to the shore, it was warm and summery, with a clear orange sunset behind the skyscrapers and soft amber fading into the blue to the east across the hazy water. Only the barest ripples splashed over the embankment. There was a feeling of great silence around, for the soft roar of the city is so steady as almost to go below consciousness. A white yacht far out near the edge of visibility was like a resting lull.
>
> But tonight! A chill, damp breeze from the north has clouded the skies and moved the waters, Instead of ripples, the embankments are awash with noisy waves, the great silence has given way to a rhythmic, pleasant, complete, deep splash of water, In another day there may be breakers! Today though, it is delicious enough to drink in the air; taste the mist on my lips, glory in the brilliant pearl-ringed lights, tingle with all my senses to the touch of the autumn night.

My conversation with Ruth and Sandy was easy and relaxed. The story of their life and how they came to live in such a way inspired me. They are peaceful, quiet people. I found I had few questions, enjoying most their honest way and the ever-present bird song. After the interview, I asked if I could travel around their woods for a couple of nights. I had brought my camping stuff. There was still three feet of snow on the ground and it was to be in the teens that night, so they were a little nervous about me bushwhacking back there. I gratefully accepted the USGS map they had tacked to the wall and set off at 4:30 P.M. I traveled mostly along frozen river beds. I had forgotten to bring a book, so silence, beauty and cold were my company, except at night when the male hoot owls called tirelessly to the females. The last time I was in the woods alone, I did battle with myself, wrestling with my psyche. This time I lolled about in my day dreams and opened my self, like Mary would, to the woods. Once, I stood listening with my eyes closed in a misty hollow below where a waterfall rumbled right under the ice. When I opened my eyes, I saw a large otter loping along his trail towards me, so intent on his journey that he did not notice me standing there. Two feet from me I called to him, "Hello Mr. Otter." Looking up, he was as shocked out of his dream world as I was. He trundled away. That night I prepared my camp well with fir boughs under my tent to keep me warmer. I cooked curried potatoes, chick-peas and onions – a gourmet feast. And I slept 14 hours and dreamed amazing dreams.

Emerging from the woods the next morning early, I felt that familiar sense of completeness and peace from spending time alone in the woods. And I thought of Mary Back and this, one of my favorite parts of the book. The book covers her entire 86 years, but it is the early days that I relate most to now. Her writing style reflects her age, 17 years old, but her spirit is infectious.

Warren Post Office
Saturday, June 28

It was just 6:30 as I ate supper – a simple, nourishing meal of cocoa, corn-meal griddle cakes fried in butter, nuts and raisins. . . .When supper was done, the dishes washed, the wipers hung up to dry on my private line, my own face and hands washed and my teeth cleaned, it was time to build up the fire with wood big enough to last, slide down into my nice warm puffy comforter, light a candle, and talk to my journal. I was proud of that candle and its reflector. The flame was perfectly sheltered and bright as can be.

My state of mind at that moment was absolutely beatific. With no vast amount of effort, and in short time, and in spite of down pouring rain, I had achieved real creature comfort. I was lying on a soft, dry bed (six inches of leaf mould is soft) with heat from a glorious fire reflected straight at me, and against the roof of my tent and down on me, good light to write by, and my tummy filled with satisfying food. Above me the wind made a million-stringed harp of the spruce tops, the stream chortled to itself below my feet, a thousand drops fell from the shaken trees – each making his tiny footstep sound. All around was the rare and tingling smell of upland forest, and my possessions all in order and all within reach. . . .It was partly pride of achievement I suppose, a new and different sort of addition to my self respect, combined with the particular exhilaration in the atmosphere. I wasn't even lonely. I was just carried out of myself with bliss. Could I have such nights, what might it not do to my daily life! Couldn't stand ′em often though. I'd burn up with white heat....

I think more than any other one thing, now that it is all over, my trip's been patterned to the rhythm of the hymn, 'Oh, worship the King, all glorious above.' . . .I have not tried to feel worshipful, but I could not help it. I am sure that God made the world, and made it so beautiful that our hearts ache to see it. . . .I think that always now, no matter how garish or drab my surroundings may be, I shall be conscious of the great, majestic beauties there are somewhere, and of the spot in my heart that's in tune with it all.

There is a spot in my heart available to me now that I am no longer working so hard to ignore my soul's longing. Sometimes it is filled with an atunement. And when I am able to submerse myself in wild nature it is there, like a low sweet hum. But other times, like the other night, the spot constricts with fear and self-doubt. I see now that maybe this is because I have been admiring my hope from afar, quietly waiting to be found out – not yet daring to really believe in it. It is different now that I have begun to build that roof and dwell inside it.

Today I have grown taller from walking
with the trees
The seven sister poplars who go
softly in a line
And I think my heart is white for
its parlay with a star
That trembled out at night and
hung above the pine.

- Mary Cooper Back, aged 17.

Our Startled Bodies

We carry red rocks
through the dark
from fire to sweat lodge
on a shovel blade,
strip, enter, and sit
pour snowmelt over the glow
and suck down the first fierce blast.
we rain our precious poisons,
amazed at how little
but water we are.

afterwards we float out
among furious stars:
sponges thoroughly wrung,
moist clay in the potter's
relentlessly gentle fist.
we fall to earth,
sleeping fitfully,
dreaming of marriage and death.

In the morning we are awakened
by our own aroma:
this irreducible mineral perfume
reminds us we've not come
so very far.

we climb down the narrow canyon,
clamber along the cliff's edge,
dive into a bottomless pool,
and our startled bodies hiss
as the hot rocks did
when the cold water hit them.

-William Clipman

I keep going back to the mountains. I like to get up on top – see what is on the other side. Look around. Even mountains I have been on top of several times. I get a hankerin' to get on top again and look 'em over.

I grew up in a wide valley, two hours' walk from the mountains. The valley had homesteads and little farms. When I was a boy, I would get up early, climb the mountains and look down on the houses of the people as they were getting up; see the smoke rise up from this farmhouse and then that one. I would go on the pretense of hunting, but most of the time I didn't want to kill anything. It was just an excuse to get away and watch people and nature doing the early morning. And I'd watch the train. It looked like a tiny worm winding through the valley.

I'd see the eagles when they were migrating in the spring and fall. They go in bunches of about a dozen. They'd glide in close to the mountains and hit the updrafts. They'd soar. They'd come in one at a time. You would think they were hunting but they were just soaring to hit the updrafts. The thermals. When they'd hit those they'd go straight up, a couple hundred feet in a couple of seconds. Their wings would be absolutely still. They'd all come in as if there was a trail, a track. Very little variation. I think they were having fun.

Living is all about enjoying what you are doing. I don't want to be tied down to something too hard. A steady job is not for me. I always had the rule that I wasn't staying on any one job more than five years. I wanted to find something else out. You get in a rut. A groove. And before long you can't get out of it.

- Ken Jones, from a Heron Dance Interview. For fifty years Ken was a mountain guide in the Canadian Rockies. I interviewed him when he was in his mid-seventies. His simplicity and happiness, his gentle smile, his contentment made a lasting impression on me.

Come dance with the west wind
and touch all the mountaintops.
Sail o'er the canyons and on to the stars.
And reach for the heavens and hope for the future,
and all that we can be, not what we are.
- John Denver, from the song, *The Eagle and the Hawk*

Soon after leaving school I heard that a new prophet had arisen among the great Zulu nation of South Africa. I was greatly excited by the news. Africa was still profoundly an Old Testament country, and the appearance of a prophet seemed not only natural and right but also an event that might always be of some cosmic importance. I went to see him as soon as I could. He lived in a round kraal, grass beehive huts on a hill standing among the complex of chasms and gorges of a deep and intricate valley in Natal. It was early summer; one of those days that come over the edge of time charged with a meaning of their own. The valley was overflowing with light, sensitive and trembling like a heart with its first apprehension of love....He was tall, dressed in a white gown that fell to his feet, and with a long staff in his hand he slowly climbed the hill towards us, as if deep in thought....

When the seer stood before us at last, raising his hand palm-outwards in the ancient Zulu greeting, I thought I had never seen a more beautiful person. His head was round and shapely, his forehead broad, his features sensitive; the face as a whole was ascetic without being either austere or fanatic. His eyes were big and well-spaced, having the look of a personality in whom nothing was hidden. His hands were those of an artist, and he used them delicately to point his words....

Outside his kraal there was a large wild fig tree whose dark green leaves were wet with light. We sat down in its shade and talked until the sun went down red behind the blue rim of the valley filled with evening smoke. The more we talked, the more I felt that I was not in the twentieth century but some early Biblical hour. We talked about a great many things of immense interest...yet about the subject that mattered most to me I was disappointed. When I begged him to speak of the first spirit of the Zulu nation, Umkuunkulu, the Great One, he shook his beautiful old head and said with infinite sadness, "We do not speak of Umkulunkulu any longer. His praise-names are forgotten. People now talk only of things that are useful to them."

Recalling this conversation, which took place nearly thirty-five years ago, I realized that the situation which I believe we are all facing in the world today was one which the primitive world, the past life of Africa, knew only too well. It is a loss of spirit, or to put it in the old-fashioned way, a loss of soul. Before my day with the Zulu prophet was over, I knew that he regarded this as the greatest calamity that could come to human beings....Indeed the primitive world regarded the preservation of first spirit as the greatest, most urgent of its tasks. It designed elaborate ritual, ceaselessly fashioned myths, legends, stories and music, to contain the meaning and feed the fire of the creative soul.

- Laurens Van Der Post, from *The Heart of the Hunter*

Those who are hunting birds destroy their chances of seeing many when they hang to a fixed schedule. Birds warm to idlers better than to the important people who bustle along the road and trail with a preoccupied expression on their faces. We had a substantial breakfast that morning, what with oatmeal, griddlecakes, bacon, crackers fried in the fat, and coffee. But the birds singing in the tree tops, swinging in the sunshine, and calling to one another in clear tones drew us away from our meal more than once...

We had seen no one since leaving Chocorua on Monday noon. But now as we approached camp we found it already occupied by two lads cooking the last of their supper. Their greeting was as cordial as though we were old acquaintances. They had been at work for the past month on the trails leading up Paugus, Passaconaway and Whiteface, and had improved all the paths save the Walden Path over which we had come that afternoon.

We set about splitting wood at once; and as night crept down over the mountain and the only light came from the dancing flames, we finished supper and laid out our beds. Then all four sat down close to the fire and compared notes – not merely of the woods, but of those larger subjects of life with which all mortals concern themselves. Such meetings are explorations, intellectual adventures, in search of common ground. And what joy it is to discover behind strange features and strange voices the old landmarks of comradeship. It was not merely that these new friends liked to sleep and cook in the open and loved the trees and mountains where they worked all day. Beyond all this they, too, were concerned with life, were eager to know what was false and what true, were on the watch for beauty and kept the windows of their look-outs clean lest something of value escape them. They had their fields for observation, as we had ours, for no man can watch the entire landscape. But for all that the principles are constant, and it is rare to find two whose fields have not overlapped. And so by the time our firewood was gone and the flames had become spasmodic, we all knew roughly what property we had in common and what each held in his own right. It is the virtue of intellectual property that all may profit by what one holds alone, and no matter what demands are made upon it the owner is none the poorer.

- Brooks Atkinson, from *Skyline Promenades* (1925).

Blue sky. I am eight years old, lying on my back on the ground in the woods. I lie there and stare for two or three hours at the mashed potato clouds and their changing forms as they drift by overhead.

One afternoon, about twenty-five years later, I was driving north to canoe for a week in Canada's Algonquin Park. I stopped by my parents' house in Ottawa, and as I was leaving, I overheard my dad say to one of his old army buddies, "He lives for these trips." That surprised me. I am not even sure I had yet come to completely realize how much those one-week solo trips, which I found time to take only every year or two, had come to be the center of my life. I was surprised he had seen that. I got in my car, waved and drove off. I have never mentioned it to him, but I think often of that offhand comment of his.

On the surface, I was in my early thirties, had a young family and was working in the investment business. On the surface, my dad was the administrative head of the counter-espionage, counter-terrorist unit of the Canadian government. We've had lots of ups and down, my dad and I, and yet maybe we understand more about each other than we let on.

Thirty-six or so hours later, I was sitting beside a lake that was shrouded in a gray, pre-dawn fog. I had gotten up in the dark, packed my canoe, and was sitting out at the shore sipping tea. Two loons drifted in and out of view. One stretched and called that haunting call of the wild.

Four years later I had to spend one week every couple of months in a hospital getting experimental chemotherapy. I would lie in the hospital bed, close my eyes, and see and hear that lake and those loons. The actual experience lasted perhaps twenty seconds, but it sustained me through hours and months.

Perhaps each human life is fed by the underground spring of a few experiences. When we are there, we touch something beyond words. Four such experiences come to my mind. Perhaps there have been a few more. They make me who I am to me, who I am under the personas I assume to negotiate my way in the world.

It amazes me how often in my life I have embarked upon work, upon commitments that have absorbed years of effort, that have nothing whatever to do with those moments of deep peace and joy. In fact, I can say that I have spent most of my life living as if I was trying to prove that those moments don't matter. At the age of forty-four I think that my life has been about a very few precious experiences.

- Rod MacIver

The beagles are going home along the small hill lanes, the huntsmen tired, the followers gone, the hare safe in its form. The valley sinks into mist, and the yellow orbital ring of the horizon closes over the glaring cornea of the sun. The eastern ridge blooms purple, then fades to inimical black. The earth exhales into the cold dusk. Frost forms in hollows shaded from the afterglow. Owls wake and call. The first stars hover and drift down. Like a roosting hawk, I listen to silence and gaze into the dark.

- J.A. Baker, from *The Peregrine*

Do not stand at my grave and weep
I am not there. I do not sleep.

I am a thousand winds that blow.
I am the diamond glint on snow.

I am the sunlight on ripened grain.
I am the gentle autumn rain.

When you wake in the morning bush
I am the swift, uplifting rush
of quiet birds in circling flight.
I am the soft starlight at night.

Do not stand at my grave
and weep.
I am not there. I do not sleep.

- Anonymous

Recommended Reading

Of the many books read and excerpted for this issue, we would particularly like to draw your attention to the following:

Atchafalaya Autumn by Greg Guirard: Some of the paintings in this issue were inspired by the beautiful photographs of *Atchafalaya Autumn*. It is truly a work of love. As author/photographer Guirard says, "There is no place on Earth where I feel more at peace than in the great Atchafalaya Basin of South Central Louisiana. This book is largely a result of my attempt to return to the woods of my childhood, the Atchafalaya Basin of my youth. I was bound to fail, of course, since that young boy and that place and time are gone now..."

Greg Guirard's book can be ordered by contacting him at 337-394-4631, 1470-A Bayou Mercier Road, St. Martinsville, LA 70582.

Birds In Art: Each year I order this catalog of paintings and sculptures produced by the Leigh Yawkey Woodson Art Museum (700 North Twelfth Street, Wausau, WI 54403, 715-845-7010). The works in these books have inspired a number of watercolors reproduced in HERON DANCE over the years.

Jayber Crow by Wendell Berry: A novel of life in small-town America before and during the transition into mechanized farming. Wendell Berry, a poet and author of several books, both fiction and non-fiction, has been identified with the environmental movement but is often critical of that movement. Jayber Crow is about the simpler life of pre-industrial agriculture, and it is about a way of life centered around community, despite the challenges and flaws of that community. Unrequited love, life without ambition, a life centered around a river and around friends are the central themes of this important, beautifully written book.

Kindred Spirits by Lorrie Harrison: This book, published by Island Time Press, profiles 32 people living on a small island community in the Pacific Northwest. It is a beautifully designed, large format book that succeeds because of Lorrie Harrison's passion for the project, her easy, heartfelt writing and gentle and honest interviewing. The 32 people represent a diversity of outlook, age and interests surprising for such a small community.

The Legacy of Luna by Julia Butterfly Hill: I read this book a year after it first came out. I thought I *should* read it, but I just could not imagine how I could get through 738 days of living in a tree. But, I was suprised to find that I was captivated by Julia's story of her stay in the tree she named *Luna*. Her voice is unusually honest and unapologetically direct. She is able to relate deeply personal and powerful experiences without sounding trite or forced. I finished the book filled with admiration and respect for her courage and clarity of purpose.

Maya Lin, A Strong Clear Vision: A video about the work of the woman who designed the Vietnam Veterans Memorial while attending Yale. The film documents a young architectural student's tenacity and persistence with her artistic vision in the face of criticism. The film can be obtained from the American Film Foundation, www.americanfilmfoundation.com, 310-459-2116.

New Jersey Owls by Len Soucy: The quote on page 45 is from an interview I did of Len seven or so years ago. Len recently published a book of photographs, drawings and observations on owls – a book I would recommend as a reference source to anyone interested in the subject. His book can be purchased through The Raptor Trust, 1390 White Bridge Road, Millington, NJ 07946.

The Peregrine by J.A. Baker: A powerfully written account by a man who for ten winters studied peregrines near his home along England's coast. Although it is prose, much of the book reads like a poem. The book is repetitive: the weather, the peregrine is spotted, the peregrine soars, the peregrine hunts, the peregrine kills, the peregrine eats. He talks of thinking like them and imitating them, and of the dislike of humans he shares with them. His love becomes an obsession that borders on the fanatical:

> I found myself crouching over the kill, like a mantling hawk. My eyes turned quickly about, alert for the walking heads of men. Unconsciously I was imitating the movements of a hawk, as in some primitive ritual; the hunter becoming the thing he hunts. I looked into the wood. In a lair of shadow the peregrine was crouching, watching me, gripping the neck of a dead branch. We live, in these days in the open, the same ecstatic fearful life. We shun men. We hate their suddenly uplifted arms, the insanity of their flailing gestures, their erratic scissoring gait, their aimless stumbling ways, the tombstone whiteness of their faces.

The Solace of Open Spaces by Gretel Ehrlich: This collection of essays based on Ehrlich's experiences as a Wyoming ranch hand and sheepherder, contradicted many of the ideas I have held about cowboys and ranch life. Her powers of observation and keen insight into human nature drew me in. Her writing is direct, stark and sensual.

Totem Salmon by Freeman House: On one level, this is a book about efforts to restore a salmon run to a small river in northern California. On another, it is a story about a community of ranchers, loggers, fisherman, old hippies and pot growers who try to find a way to work together based on the common, if often uncomfortable, belief that salmon are important to the place they call home. The book explores the notion that the commitment we make to something outside ourselves costs us and changes us, but is ultimately where the real richness of life is found.

Bulletin Board

Website Update

We've made a number of changes to our website. We can now take orders on our SECURE SITE for renewals, new and gift subscriptions, notecards, art, videos, posters, t-shirts and donations. In addition, we have uploaded our new notecards, limited edition art, t-shirts, poster and a selection of our watercolors (in color).

Extra Copies of the Fall Issue of Heron Dance

Due to a 25% increase in postal costs this year and increased printing costs, we cannot afford to give two extra free copies of the fall issue to the subscribers who requested them. We are able to offer extra copies of issue #32 to subscribers for $3.00 each, over 50% off the retail price. Please contact us to order these extra copies.

Automatic Renewals

To subscribers who have e-mail, we now offer an automatic renewal service. Each year, on the expiration of your subscription, we charge your credit card for your subscription, minus a two-dollar discount as a thank-you for the time, paper and postage this saves us.

To sign up, send us a credit card number with at least a year to run before it expires. Each year we will notify you by e-mail that we intend to charge your account or card in two weeks. At any time you may cancel this arrangement.

Mailing List Exchanges, Rentals, Donations

In order to build a subscriber base that can sustain Heron Dance, we continue to send out our flyers to potential subscribers. To make this effort financially viable we trade or rent our subscriber list. If you would rather we did not include your name and address in these trades or rentals, please advise us by phone, mail or e-mail.

In addition, the Direct Marketing Association can place your name on a no-mail list, reducing your unwanted mail by 80 percent. Contact the Direct Marketing Association at PO Box 9008, Farmingdale, NY 11735, 212-768-7277.

Videos

We offer two of Frederic Back's incredible videos: ***The Man Who Planted Trees*** and ***The Mighty River,*** at a cost of $20 each, shipping included. Frédéric Back's work has been a major inspiration to Heron Dance.

Back Issues

Heron Dance offers an anthology of the first 25 issues for $68 (530 pages). Issues 26 to 30 are available for $30. A complete set of back issues is $90.

Heron Dance T-Shirts

Our 100% organic t-shirts are available for $15 each, shipping included. Sizes S, M, L and XL. A watercolor graphic of a howling wolf graces the back with the words: In celebration of the Great Mystery.

Dear Readers,

There was a night about six weeks ago when Rod and I were walking down the dirt road near our house. Issue 30 had just gone in the mail and we felt suspended by the tight energy of expectancy. Rod predicted incorrectly *again* when spring would actually come. Then we tried silence. In the end, there was just no way around the waiting and wondering. The changes in issue 30 reflected who we really are – our love of wild nature. Soon 11,000 people would have that in their hands.

Two days later the tightness left. Before any feedback came in, we felt at peace with the changes, realizing that putting forth the truest part of ourselves was the best we could do – the only thing we could do. It was a mutual exhale.

Several weeks later we sent out our appeal letter. Feeling deep gratitude for the many donations and extra purchases was predictable. What was not, was how such generosity would affect us. Your support means more to us than financial survival.

Rod, Doreen, Pamela and I thank you. Anyone lacking faith in humanity should hear the phone calls we get and read the beautiful messages. We consider ourselves deeply privileged.

In celebration of the Great Mystery,

Ann Rod.

Ann and Rod

Recently, we sent out an appeal for money to get us through some lean times. Thanks to the generous support of the following people and many more who will be thanked in the next issue, Heron Dance continues its celebration of the Great Dance of Life.

Saul Ader
Adriann Alcalde
Nancy and Allan Anderson
Ron Alexander & Lorrie Devirian
Elsie Allbright
Bill Allen
Tim and Lucia Amsden
Anonymous
Elizabeth Armenta
Betty Armstrong
Cheryl Ashmore
Beth Avner
Joan Babcock
Alan Baron
Emanuel Batler
Duane Beard
Kristie Beasley
Chris Bein
Carl Bellini
Bennu
Father Tom Berry
Mary Bione
Samuel Bland
Mary Blizzard
Barry Bloom
Stuart Bromberg
Dana Carman
Elizabeth M. Cheatham
Ray Chevraux
Peter Clark
John Compher
Joe and Donna Cooper
Joey Corcoran
Ann Crossman
Michael and Marcia Cummings
Dr. and Mrs. William Daily
Jean Dalenburg
John Daubney
Ann Day
Melodee Dew
John DeWitt
Mary Dick
Janice Digirolamo
Anne Disarcina
Elizabeth Demontigny
Tom and Denise DiGiovanni
Delta Donohue
Mary Alice Dooley
David Drake
Dr. Karl Duff
Lois Duke
Bob Duncan
Paula Eder
Buck Elliot
Jim Farfaglia
Mark Feinknopf & Cynthia Moe
Adela Feran
Stuart Fraser
Vic Fritterman
Julie Forrest
Michael Fostyk
Sam Fuller
Peter Gallant
Shirley Galliher
Cynthia Giannini
Bill Gish
Dr. Clare Gnecco
Dagmar Goldschmidt
Carole Grey-Whiting
Margo Coffin Groff
Jim Guinness
Greg Guirard
Pamela Halbakken
Mary Haley
Joan Hamel
Jane and John Handy
Susan Hargrave
Jerry Harper
Lorrie Harrison
Dr. Gordon Hasick
Mr. and Mrs. David Hawkins
Mel Heiman
Maurice and Artye Hellner
Rebecca Henderson
Harriet Hight
Ken Hitzig
Warren Hohwald
Carol Hosmer
Carol Hovey
Will Inman
Donald Janak
Charlotte Jones
Jun Jones
Mary Kealoha
Thomas Kelahan
Mary Kelly

Rosemary Kemp
Mary Kincaid
Carole Kirouac
Henry Klug
Carol Knox
Frank Kurhayez
Bruce Ladd
Debbie Landes
Debbie Lanford
Susan Lantz
Lisa Larkin
Jacqulyn Lazzell
The Leppert Family
Barbara Lewis
Dean Lloyd
Robin Lloyd
Nancy Lovejoy
Jennifer McAlevy (in honor of her mom, Kathryn McAlevy)
Catherine McCall
Thomas McGrady
John P. McLaughlin
James McLeer
Nina Manzi
Margo Martens
Nancy and Marty Mazzanti
Minerva Medina
B. Micetich
Amanda Moore
Bonnie Morton
Michael Mowers
Monica Munaretto
Helen Nannicini
Dorothy Nelligan
Kenneth Nickerson
Hethea Nye
Jane O'Neill
Winnie O'Shaughnessy
Ron Palmer
Michael Parvaneh
Neal Peck
Albert Pohl
A. Alex Porter
Sue Reamer
Monica Relph-Wikman
Carolyn Reynolds
Jane Richardson
Susan Roe
Fred Rogers
Eileen Romano
Cordelia Middleton Rorrick
Paul and Linda Saccone
Mary Ann Sanders
Sheri Sather
Linda and Patrick Sedlacek
Mike Schroeder
Leo Senneville
Dan Serebrakian
David Shepard
Robert Shuman
Paula Sidle
Edward and Elizabeth Sims
Robert Sittig
Harold A. Smith
Beverly Sorenson
John Squadra
Mary Stewart
Cathy Stone
Brian Strock
Teresa and Fritz Stumpges
Timberlake Farms
Elisabeth Taylor
Michael Tebbe
Rene Thomas
Terry Tinkle
Tom Todd
Tedra Towne
Mrs. Donald Turk
Virginia Vollmer
Mary Waddington
Kees Wagenvoord
John and Anne Wagner
Tom Wagner
Robert Walker
Thomas Waller
Janice Wallace
Brian Weld
Well of Mercy
Jennifer Wells
Sarah Wesson
Frederick Whitmeyer
Dr. Jim Wilson
Powell Woodward
Marian Worgul
Carol Wright
Jean Zelazny

Heron Dance notecards: New notecards are now available in a gift box. We offer 20 different cards; one is pictured above. The cost is $22 including shipping.
Heron Dance watercolors: The originals of the art in Heron Dance are available at a cost of $75 to $200 each depending on size, which ranges from 8" by 11" to 22" by 30." All prices include shipping.
Limited Edition Prints: Limited edition, signed prints of the image on page one are available at a cost of $50 (10" x 15") and $100 (20" x 30"). Each image is limited to 50 prints and is printed on the same high-quality watercolor paper as the original, using the Gicleé process. The original is available for $300.